THE SPIRIT OF SCOTLAND

THE SPIRIT OF SCOTLAND

JAMES S. ADAM

THE RAMSAY HEAD PRESS EDINBURGH

First published in 1977 by
The Ramsay Head Press
36 North Castle Street
Edinburgh EH2 3BN

Printed in Great Britain by
Macdonald Printers (Edinburgh) Limited
Edgefield Road, Loanhead, Midlothian

CONTENTS

To
Ailish and Ian
and those who will follow

INTRODUCTORY

IT is not easy to be objective or dispassionate when writing about one's own country and people. Indeed, I have found it impossible and have not made the attempt. Rather I have stressed the qualities which have seemed to me to be important national characteristics: pride of race is one; a sense of adventure is another; a natural concept of democracy and an instinctive egalitarianism are two more; surprisingly, perhaps to some, there is also a basic humility.

True, we are all familiar with the story of the man whose prayer was, "An' Lord, gie me a guid conceit o' masel," an aspiration in a Scot which many would regard as superfluous, a work of super-erogation, but which, north of the Border, is understood to be a proper desire for a proper conceit properly founded on achievement.

When we look at the national record, we see some of the basis for that pride. Duns Scotus was an early philosopher who was followed by David Hume and Thomas Carlyle. James Bruce, Mungo Park and David Livingstone were early courageous explorers. Captain James Cook, the great seaman explorer, was the son of a Scottish farmworker. James Watt demonstrated to the world the power of steam and triggered off the Industrial Revolution. John Napier of Merchiston invented logarithms. Alexander Graham Bell gave us the telephone. James "Paraffin" Young found out how to get oil out of shale and started the world's oil technology. Dr James Young Simpson introduced chloroform and took the pain and terror out of medicine and surgery; his chloroform was provided for him by Duncan Flockhart from a chemist's shop at the west end of Princes Street, Edinburgh. John

Logie Baird pioneered television. Robert Watson Watt developed radar. Alexander Fleming discovered penicillin. Mary Slessor, a Dundee mill girl, became a missionary and was acclaimed as the "White Queen of Okoyong."

Sir Walter Scott and Robert Louis Stevenson chose to write much of their dialogue in Scots but nevertheless (or perhaps because of that) their books and poems had and have a world following. Robert Burns expressed in simple and memorable terms mankind's hopes and feelings and expressed them so movingly that his work has universal recognition. Indeed, it is probably true to say that one of his songs, "Auld Lang Syne," is sung in more countries of the world than is any other song.

At a time when England had only two universities, Scotland had four. The Scottish educational system is still a long way ahead of England's in its insistence on highly-qualified, trained, graduate teachers and in its traditional provisions for pushing on the lad o' pairts.

There are fewer barriers for women; it was in Scotland that Margaret Kidd became the first woman in Britain to take silk to become an advocate and Queen's Counsel. Scotland can also claim Helen Smellie of Glasgow as the first woman to be accepted as a member of the Stock Exchange. It is also true to say that married women in Scotland had property and inheritance protection by law, several generations before their sisters in England began to catch up.

Having got thus far, the reader who is prepared to go on will understand that what follows is a one-sided, hopelessly-biased, purely-personal account of Scotland and the Scots. It is personal in that it is based on the people I know and have gladly encountered in various ploys; it is an expression of proper conceit in my country and my compatriots in which

I have tried to emphasise a native sense of adventure both physical and intellectual.

So much of what I have written is derived from what I have read and heard over the years that I would find it difficult and invidious to try to attribute every point or item but some explanations may be helpful. The verse heading chapter four is from Ecclesiastes, the verse heading chapter six is from Byron, and the verses heading chapters one and five are imitative but my own; for those readers who may be interested, I ought to say that the verse for chapter five is written to the rhythm of the marching song of Clan Macintyre—*Gabhaidh Sinn an Rathad Mor*.

The Gaelic quotation which heads the final chapter is taken from the memorial at Fortingall to General Stewart of Garth, the Historian of the Highland Regiments, from which history so much else has been quarried.

I must, however, acknowledge specially the verse which introduces chapter three. The poem from which I have borrowed it was written by Alastair MacTavish Dunnett in 1930. It seemed to me then and it seems to me today to be a vigorous example of the imaginative talent of a man who has one of the most brilliant minds in contemporary Scotland. I gladly take this opportunity to acknowledge the pleasure and profit that I have derived from my close association with him over many happy years and experiences covering both personal and business adventures.

Since returning to Edinburgh in October 1975, I happily found myself involved in my most satisfying personal and business adventure to date. Towards the end of that year, I was invited to become Organiser for the International Gathering of the Clans 1977. It was an invitation which I accepted with alacrity for, monumental though the task was, it brought me back into close contact with many valued friends and colleagues. It also afforded me the rare privilege of serving as the key link man between the home Scot and the international Scot. A rare privilege, indeed. It put me to the awesome challenge of being the instrument through which people of my race and blood were brought together in a way never before achieved, or attempted. It was a task to be approached with pride and with a due humility. I have never believed that "mountains divide us, and the waste of seas." We were and are a people of the hills and the seas that separate can also provide the path to fresh unities; I hope that I may have helped to achieve a strengthening of the bonds of clanship.

CHAPTER ONE

Where'er a man goes
With himself for crew,
Whate'er that man wills,
That task he can do.

COME with me first to the west and to the isles of the Hebrides. There you will meet colour in the landscape and in the sea; you will be captivated by the character of the people who live and travel there. Let me introduce you to the very special quality of our western seaboard through some of those who give that entrancing sunset shore its life, its legend, and its constant romantic appeal.

It was a wet wild windy day in early winter and the old *S.S. Hebrides* was nosing her way into Uig Bay in the Isle of Skye. As we passed close into a headland, there on the edge of the rocks two young boys with home-made rods were fishing in the stormy seas. Captain MacKinnon, a Skyeman himself, expressed his local pride to those around. The boys from Skye had the right stuff, he said; the stock was still good. "They're hardy," he declared. It was an encomium you will hear often in the Highlands, and if you want to know precisely what it means you must go, as in the case of so many of the other words used there, to French. Its soupçon comes straight from the Auld Alliance. It derives from *hardi* and it is a tribute to youthful audacity rather more than to physical toughness.

17

Captain MacKinnon, along with many of his colleagues, has long gone to Tir nan Og, and the old *Heb* to the breaker's yard, but the memory of some of that remarkable crew remains. Alastair MacRae, the wireless operator, is still happily engaging in his hobby of ornithology. His twin enthusiasms for piping and ornithology were shared by the crew. During many a stormy winter passage, occasional skirls from his pipes would be snatched by the gale and carried to the bridge where they were heard with appreciative smiles. It seemed perfectly natural that the second officer should break off a conversation, dash to the voice pipe, and say, "MacRae. There's a bird 300 yards off the starboard bow. What is it?" And Alastair would down his pipes, grab his binoculars, whip out of his cabin, and give the identification.

That period was in the early thirties and I made full use of the *S.S. Hebrides* for personal travel and also for taking a group of young boys from a poor district of Glasgow adventuring round the isles. Not only was it an adventure. It was cheap forby. From Glasgow to Skye, via the Outer Hebrides and St Kilda. Eight to ten days' tramp steaming for 15 shillings. That was for travelling steerage, of course, cooking our food on the crew's half of the galley.

There were cabins for 12 first-class passengers and a splendid old-fashioned mahogany saloon for the privileged dozen. In the early days, an envious aspiration to travel first class was firmly rebuked by one of the crew—"You wouldn't want to be travelling with them, would you?"

Latterly I did travel with "them" largely because it was lonely to be the only passenger forward in the steerage during the cold rough days of winter. But one missed the close contact with the crew, Gaelic speakers on the deck and Glaswegians in the engine room.

One of the greasers, a squat bow-legged Glaswegian with a face plain to the point of ugliness but who had a heart of pure gold used to come and see me as I lay in my sleeping bag on one of the steerage benches, regal in my solitude. He would say with a craggy toothless grin, "Ah'll be comin' aff at fower in the moarnin' an' Ah'll be makin' a cup o' tea; wid ye like me tae bring ye ane in yer scratcher." I always said yes and he would say, "Mind, Ah'll waken ye." He always did. I didn't really want the tea and I didn't really want to be wakened, especially if the ship happened to be pitching or rolling, which it usually was in the winter, but it was a kindly thought on his part and I enjoyed the crack with him, which went on until he would say, "Ah'm aff tae ma scratcher."

Another of the engine-room crew was a Stewart and he knew what that meant and if he thought you did not he would tell you of the Clan motto, "Royal is my name and royal is my race." It was an experience to talk to him when he came up to the deck for a breather and a smoke. He would stand just inside the half-door in his singlet and dungarees with a sweat-rag round his neck, his eyes faded and blood shot from the heat of the stokehold and would talk with enthusiasm of the Jacobites and Prince Charlie, as if he too had been there. "It's been known, mind you, for footsoldiers to stand the charge of mounted troops," he told me. "It's been known. But it wasn't known for footsoldiers to charge mounted troops. But the Jacobites did it at Prestonpans and the battle was over in seven minutes fifty seconds."

Not very accurate history but there was no mistaking his pride of race and royal clan as he expounded his passionate credo while we steamed the seas of the Hebrides where the fugitive prince found shelter and courageous loyalties.

There is in most Scots such a sense of history and clanship

that time is often blurred. During the War, the S.O.E.—the Special Operations Executive—conducted their field training around Loch Morar. My old friend, Major Bob Millar, who was one of the first officers to be picked for S.O.E., told me this fascinating story of how history and the war came together. From time to time the operatives were taken into the hills at the head of the loch and left there to find their way back. Because of danger to their families in occupied Europe, the security instructions were explicit. Operatives were to use and be addressed by their code names at all times. Well, of course, that instruction was frequently forgotten and real names were used in the hearing of the local boatman who ferried the groups on the loch. The Colonel decided that he had better have a word about security with the boatman just to make sure that names did not slip out over a drink in the bar of the Morar Hotel. He explained carefully in simple terms how important it was that conversation should be guarded and that there should be no possibility of information about the operatives leaking out of the area. When he had finished his lecture on elementary security, the boatman said simply, "You don't need to worry, Colonel. We had a Prince up here with £30,000 on his head and nobody gave him away."

It was then almost two hundred years since the Prince had been there and the reward was offered, but to the boatman it was his Prince and his people who had been involved and he was a part of that living history.

The highlight of these tours of the Hebrides was undoubtedly the landing on St Kilda. If we had no concept of the hazards, the nervousness of the captain and the comments of the crew as weather checks were intensified during the approach eventually made us all aware that anchoring off a beach open squarely to the prevailing wind was not approved. To underline the

20

message, we were told that if the weather was likely to blow up we would not be permitted to land and that, furthermore, if we were permitted to land and the weather blew up, the *S.S. Hebrides* would up anchor and leave us until the weather settled. When we steamed into the bay we were met by one of the Fergusons rowing out to meet us. For some years after the evacuation of St Kilda in the thirties, Ferguson senior, who was a native of the island and who had a tweed business in Glasgow, used to go with some of his family each year to pluck the wool from the agile St Kildan sheep which became wilder each year and which could jump over a man's head. Each year he made a weaving of the hard tough St Kildan tweed.

Alastair MacRae, who knew young Ferguson well, tongue in cheek, shouted a courteous greeting in Gaelic to him and was answered in Glasgow idiom. "Away," replied young Ferguson, "and pipeclay up the lum." It was an equally authentic voice of the west and if you do not understand the futility which that phrase describes, just ask the nearest Glaswegian.

We were lucky and were allowed enough time ashore to explore the island, to walk along the deserted main street of the village with its sixteen houses, to look at the cleits of stone in which the St Kildans dried their hay, and to climb to the top of the Conagher. From there we looked down into the Atlantic at the bottom of the highest sea cliff in Britain descending sheer into deep water. It was on the cliffs around the group of islands that the St Kildans won their food. They were all expert and fearless cragsmen whose main task was to bring back young fulmars for oil, gulls for their feathers, and young gannets for food. Before a young St Kildan took a wife, for whom he would have to scale the cliffs in earnest,

21

he proved his head for heights by standing on one leg on a stone high over the sea. So far as I know, all the young St Kildan men survived the test to get themselves safely married.

One of the fascinating qualities of journeying in the Hebrides is the way in which the whole of the west coast and the islands shrinks to become like a village in character. People who live hundreds of miles apart know of each other and behave like near neighbours. One such who endeared himself to all who met him was the late James C. MacPhee. Jimmie—a native of Ballachulish, a slate village on Loch Leven and which he used to describe half-jocularly as the "loveliest village in the Highlands"—latterly lived and worked in London, which he treated as a village. He took me once to discuss a project with Kenneth Campbell, the then Managing Director of the British and India Steamship Company. That visit was followed by a call on the shoeblack in the Westbury Hotel in New Bond Street. Jimmie was interested in both as persons and each recognised this and responded to it, for Jimmie had the great gift of conveying his own gusty enthusiasm for living. He also made a number of people in London interested in Gaelic and in Gaelic song. He had himself a beautiful tenor voice which had earned him a gold medal at one of the Mods. At this particular time I was editing the *Weekly Scotsman* to which Jimmie contributed first a column and latterly a page weekly. He was an engineer and draughtsman and had no formal training in journalism but he brought his rare gift of human interest to his writing as well as to his living. Jimmie's weekly page became a subject of some envy and the London Editor of *The Scotsman* office advised me that he had had queries from the Fleet Street N.U.J. (National Union of Journalists) about Jimmie's activities and that there could be claims that the page should be done by a member. I put it in writing that the job was open but that there were certain pre-requisites: "Candidates should be Scottish or of Scottish descent and prepared to attend Caledonian functions in the London area seven nights a week, that preferably they should be Gaelic speakers and that it would count strongly in their favour if they had won a gold medal at the Mod thirty years ago." I don't know how much of my reply was passed on but that was the last I heard of that particular piece of nonsense.

Some of the junior officers in the 4/5 Camerons T.A. were working in London and those who were in the Islands Company had Gaelic speakers under them and Jimmie encouraged them in their learning of Gaelic. They included the Earl of Dunmore, MacDonald of Clanranald and Rory MacDonald. Johnnie Dunmore is now working in public relations in Glasgow, Rory MacDonald has the Clachaig Inn, Glencoe, and is also marketing a 100 proof malt whisky under the name of Glencoe. Rory made the newspaper and radio headlines a year or two back by refusing to accommodate Campbells in the Clachaig. He explained: "A man is entitled to his prejudices and, you know, we had Campbells as guests here before and they behaved rather badly."

Jimmie arranged with the Scottish BBC to organise a ceilidh by the Islands Company at an annual camp at Folkestone, and tutored MacDonald of Clanranald in "Morag of Dunvegan." Clanranald is a big boisterous chap who some day could well resemble Compton MacKenzie's "Ben Nevis." He complained to Jimmie that the "damned blobs" of the staff notation were confusing, so Jimmie wrote the music in stress form. Clanranald then declared of the chorus, *Ho bhan 's na ho bhan o*, "I can't get that first 'haow' quite right." And that was no exaggeration. He couldn't get the second or third right either and his singing was atrocious. In the event, someone at the ceilidh sang "Morag of Dunvegan" before Clanranald could get at it and he was forced back on to a a Gaelic nursery rhyme song which he rendered excruciatingly but with enthusiasm. It was gallant and the hit of the evening.

Jimmie made full use of that song. At another dinner, he called on the young MacLeod of MacLeod, whose family seat is at Dunvegan, to sing "Morag" in which Jimmie had been coaching him. MacLeod was taken aback, but he got up, sang it, and sang it well.

But perhaps Jimmie's greatest personal achievement was in getting Antoine Girot of Air France—a Frenchman from Normandy—interested in Gaelic to the point where he can speak, read and write in Gaelic. Antoine, who had a spell of duty in Paris, is now General Manager of Air France in the United States; and when I saw him recently he greeted me in impeccable Gaelic.

When Jimmie died, there was an impressive cross-section of friends at the Golders Green Crematorium. The service saddened me. Without a word of Gaelic, it was alien and inappropriate. Later, I was told that Jimmie's ashes were to be interred at Ballachulish. David Stephen and I went up to that little Episcopal church by the side of the loch with the hills towering over us. The tiny little hole in the ground ready to receive the urn seemed utterly inadequate to hold all that was left of that ebullience until the Minister began the funeral service. He addressed the Deity in the language that the Deity knew best in that area, and suddenly everything became fitting amongst the scenic beauty, and we were all at peace knowing that Jimmie had at last come home.

Just before he died, Jimmie underwent the operation for the removal of the larynx. He, to whom communication in laughter and song was life, faced with fortitude the problems

24

that being silenced could bring him. The day before the operation he wrote me from the Royal National Throat, Nose and Ear Hospital, Grays Inn Road, London:

Seumas, my friend,

To-morrow's the day when they aim to remove all that is troubling me. It's going to be a big job. But surrounded as I am with a wonderful aura of love and affection I feel I'll pull through all right to face what will be a new, perhaps uncomfortable, adventure in sound reproduction.

I'd just like to say *moran agus moran taing* for your kindly interest and wonderful support not only to me but to Morag. I shall never forget it.

Alastair *coir* sent me a most kindly letter. So, too, did Monty MacKenzie and a whole lot more. These I'll answer in a week or so's time.

I'm proud of my friends, of whom you are one of the greatest. Kindest regards to Flora and the family. I do hope you will have a splendid break in the Isles. You will deserve it.

Gu dileas,
Seumas.

These references to Jimmie MacPhee may seem an interpolation in an account of sailing on the *S.S. Hebrides* with its connotation of physical adventuring, but they are germane to the main concept which is that the Highlands and Islands have the friendliness and character of a far-flung village and that the physical side of living is only part of the scheme of life in which the gay and the gallant should demonstrate that adventure is also a quality of mind and spirit. It was for the latter that I most valued the journeying round the Isles on the old *S.S. Hebrides*.

But, to return to the *S.S. Hebrides.* Those leisurely journeys are not now possible. They have been priced out by rising costs and time pressures. What once would have taken ten to twelve days is now completed in six and many of the uniquely fascinating little piers and harbours are no longer points of call. We are in a new era and the old adventures have given place. But only to other kinds. Although the ships are bigger, faster, and the routes are streamlined, the sea and the islands still exercise their enduring challenge and their charm.

A few years ago I was standing on the deck of the *MV Claymore* as we entered Castlebay in Barra, the most southerly of the inhabited islands of the Outer Hebrides. The clean clear sea made a perfect foil to the blue-grey rocks, the green island with Heaval rising majestically behind the romantic pale-blue Kisimul Castle standing foursquare on its little rock in the bay.

A young man standing near me said, as much to himself as to me, "At last, I return to the land of my ancestors."

In the ensuing conversation, I learned that he was Alan MacNeill-Smith and that he, his wife and young son were making their first Hebridean journey. As I was on my way to visit the MacNeil of Barra to see how his project of rebuilding Kisimul from the ruins of the old castle was progressing, I undertook to introduce Alan and his family to their clan chief.

As a consequence, Alan rose even more strongly to the call of the blood and subsequently arranged with MacNeil that he would have a suitable herald's trumpet designed and made, to present to MacNeil for use in Kisimul Castle. The designing was not accomplished without a deal of research and striving. I can remember Alan showing me an answer he had received to a query from Sir Iain Moncreiffe of that Ilk who was then

Albany Herald, an officer in the Court of the Lyon King of Arms. Moncrieffe's answer took the form of eleven closely-written pages of foolscap illustrated in the margin with small sketches in red and blue. It ended with an apology from Moncrieffe in which he regretted that he could not provide more detail because, he said, "I am on holiday and away from my books."

When the trumpet was finally presented to MacNeil at a clan gathering in Kisimul to celebrate the restoration of the Banquetting Hall, MacNeil appointed Alan as his hereditary trumpeter. NacNeil then ate a symbolic meal to enable Alan to carry out the old clan tradition. This was for the herald to ascend the battlements and, at each of the four corners, to blow his trumpet and to cry out with a great voice the old proud boast:

"The great MacNeil of Barra has now dined. All ye princes, potentates, and rulers of the earth may now sit down."

Not so long ago, Alan had the melancholy duty of similarly telling the world that a Great MacNeil of Barra had died.

The story of Robert Lister MacNeil of Barra is the story of the bridging of two centuries. In the 18th century the MacNeil chiefs left Kisimul. The castle was burned out and then pillaged for ballast for boats. Eventually it became a picturesque ruin. Young MacNeil was born in Michigan, U.S.A., and grew up hearing the family dreams of Barra and Kisimul. He determined to buy back the estate and rebuild the castle. With that ambition to inspire him he did two significant things—he became an architect and subsequently practised in Washington, London and New York; and he established through the Lord Lyon his claim to be chief of the clan. He made a study of castles in general and Kisimul in particular. Eventually, in 1937 at the age of 47 he bought back the estate and set about restoring the castle faithfully. From then on, except for the war years, he spent his winters at his house in Marlboro, Vermont, U.S.A., and most of his summers working on the restoration of the castle. In 1959, two hundred years after his ancestor had left it, MacNeil and and his wife, Elizabeth, took up residence in the dormer house rebuilt snugly into the thick walls of the castle. He was then 69 years of age. It had taken him a lifetime but he had made his dreams come true. He has told the story himself in *Castle in the Sea* which was published by Collins in 1964.

For Alan MacNeill-Smith and his son, MacNeil's sensitive appointment brought their dreams also to life and made living an adventure. It was my privilege to have had a hand in the shaping of it.

I took my own children to see Kisimul and MacNeil. I took them also to see a road near Mallaig in Inverness-shire, for that too had its story.

A crofter, who was farming at Mallaigmor wanted to make life easier for his mother. Shopping in Mallaig by small boat was a chancy uncomfortable business so he put some stepping stones in the boggy parts of the mile or so of route by the shore of Loch Nevis but that was not really suitable either. He decided that the only thing to do was to build a road for her. It took him ten years but, single-handed, he built it—a mile-long road that runs high up on the hillside like a Himalayan track. He dug, he cut, he quarried; he went twenty, thirty feet down the hillside to pack in that twenty or thirty feet with boulders to support the track at the steepest points. Ten years, but it is there now for all so see and use, with its breathtaking views of Loch Nevis, the Sound of Sleat, and the Isle of Skye. The Army have helped to maintain it but one lonely man pioneered it, driving it onwards year after year amidst the surrounding beauty.

I wanted my children, amongst other things, to see the restored Kisimul Castle and that Mallaig road. I wanted them to sense the determination behind these achievements. I wanted to show them these physical proofs that what a man wills—he can do. I wanted them to feel for themselves the pulse of the adventure that is always there for the choosing, particularly in their own lovely, lively, challenging land of adventure.

CHAPTER TWO

Anail a' Ghaidheal, air a' mhullach.
The breathing place of the Gael is on the summit.

NO matter where you are in Scotland, you are unlikely to be far from the hills and you will certainly be able to see some of them. There they stand, a constant challenge to young blood and restless muscles, with their call to effort and their promise of rich rewards of great horizons of beauty to be viewed from their summits.

We are very lucky in that many of our cities and towns are built on or around hills. From an early age, the Scot learns to use his legs to walk upwards, a beneficial provenance which may explain why so many reach other tops in later life.

The centre of Glasgow is almost entirely built on hills, but Dundee and Edinburgh are more fortunate. Their hills can still be seen as such. Dundee Law dominates the city and the River Tay. Young Dundonians are early apprenticed to climbing the Law. I know. I was born in Dundee and I cannot remember the time when I was too young to stacher up the Law to be given the final thrill of being stood on the indicator which marks the very top. Nor, indeed, can I recollect the age at which I was excused the duty of walking a mile and a half up to the "tap o the Hilltoon" and then down the Hilltoon to kirk on Sundays. In those days of Calvinist fortitude, the introduction of the Sunday tram service was regarded as a bait by Satan to betray the weakling into supporting those who defiled the Lord's Day by working.

B   33

I well remember the delicious sense of sin and apprehension for the penalties of discovery when an uncle and I were late in setting out and he took me on the forbidden tram. His view was that it would have been even more of a public scandal had we gone into a hushed church as latecomers in a flagrant demonstration of sloth. My grandfather was not amused. Mind you, when there was snow on the ground, the Hilltoon or the equally steep Constitution Brae were both very tricky for a wee chap trying to beat the church bells which rang over the whole city.

The call of the hills is so much a pulse in the blood stream of those who have been born to them, bringing with it an appreciation of the fervour with which psalmist and poet wrote of them, that it is a shattering experience to meet a man who has neither the grandeur of the hills nor the beauty of language in his soul. At the beginning of the war, I had the task of conducting a celebrated American columnist around Glasgow, the Clyde and the West of Scotland. It was before America entered the war and my columnist baffled me by taciturnity. I could not get him to talk on any subject. I came to the conclusion that he must have been suspicious of me, and fearful lest I pump him full of British propaganda. It was Alastair Dunnett's task to take the same columnist around the Edinburgh area and I later compared experiences. He had contrived to get a positive response. It was even more shattering than the silences. On the ramparts of Edinburgh Castle, looking around from that historic setting to the stimulating prospect, Alastair quoted some appropriate verse. "Poetry," declared the columnist flatly, "is just a roundabout way of saying something which can be expressed much better in prose." He had been born on the plains, we learned, and it seemed to us that, having never in his youth lifted his eyes to the hills, he had also lacked the early impulse to lift his soul to the high peaks of language and imagination.

I thought of my grandfather in his middle age going off from his family to Donside—there to climb the hill of Bennachie, to set his foot on the top of the hill he had first seen as a wee laddie. Unlike the columnist, my grandfather never travelled physically outside of Scotland, apart from one holiday in London and another in Newcastle. Poverty denied him the opportunity but he had the greater gift of mind—a gift which enabled him to know that growing up "where the Gadie rins at the back o' Bennachie" made it possible for him to see over the hills and far away. Incidentally, although my grandfather left school early and worked at the age of eight in a Dundee factory it was on his lips that I first heard Burns quoted. He also referred to his open or "cut-throat" razor as his Andrea Ferrara. Long afterwards I used to wonder about these references which I am sure he had not read but must have heard. I wondered at the oral tradition which led him to speak of his razor as though it was one with the claymores of the Jacobites, who prized most the blades made by Andrea Ferrara, swordsmith.

There were many things I would have liked to ask him when it was too late but I did ask him if he remembered any reaction to tartan. Only once, he told me. He was seventeen and had bought himself a red tartan cravat before going to see his grandmother on Donside. What the clan of the tartan was he did not know but his grandmother knew. "What," she asked severely, "are you daein' wi' a Stewart on?" It offended her to see her grandson wearing a tartan other than his own. That visit was around 1869 and put his grandmother's roots back to around 1800. One other recollection of that time which clearly gave my teetotal grandfather great personal pleasure was that he remembered seeing his aunts preparing to go into Aberdeen market with half mutchkins of whisky under their top skirts. A little bit of private distilling was obviously part of the local and family tradition—a birthright as it were. I feel it only honest at this point to give a fair warning to the Excise that just as an Englishman feels it a native right to brew himself some beer or cider so too do I feel about my *uisge beatha*. I feel impelled to claim my birthright, and sometime, before the divot is at my mouth, I must engage in a little adventure with barley mash, peat and a still in the heather. The result may not be potable but the adventure will assuredly be spirited.

From the top, Dundee Law commands as fair a prospect as can be seen anywhere. The Sidlaw Hills, the Central Highlands, the hills of Fife, the North Sea, and a wee keek of St Andrews. In the forefront is the silvery Tay, surely one of the world's loveliest rivers. It is said that when some venturesome Romans (and there were not many who ventured north from the safety of Antonine's Wall which ran from the Clyde to the Forth) pushed north and got their first glimpse of the Tay, they exclaimed, "Ecce Tiber." Sir Walter Scott put that piece of nonsense into perspective with an exquisite Caledonian rebuttal:

> "Behold the Tiber!" the vain Roman cried
>   viewing the ample Tay from Baiglie's side.
> But where's the Scot that would the vaunt repay
>   and hail the puny Tiber for the Tay?

One of the consequences of seeing other faraway hills from the top of the Law is the birth of the desire to climb these others and to know what hidden delights lie on the far sides. They are there demanding to be climbed and that is the mountaineer's justification for his conquest of the great peaks, but he starts with the wee hills at his back door.

Edinburgh's Arthur's Seat is a more massive lump of a hill but it has the merit of being much closer to the heart of the city. When I worked at *The Scotsman*, Alastair Dunnett and I used to make a point of meeting in a climb to the top of Arthur's Seat before going into the office to start the day's work. There must be few cities where one can hear the mountain lark in the clear air of the day, see a greylag goose, or watch a stoat roll an egg across the road. From the top of Arthur's Seat, as with Dundee Law, there is another stimulating view especially to the north west where the Highland hills stand blue and enticing, calling those who would refresh themselves on their summits.

Once a year, Edinburgh students stage a race up Arthur's Seat. It is a tough run for the fit but also once a year the Reverend Ronnie Selby-Wright, minister of the historic Canongate Kirk, used to lead a gathering to the top to hold a dawn May Day service attended by people of all ages, a task now undertaken by one of the younger ministers. There, in the morning mists, they worship the God who created both them and the everlasting hills. There, they look down on the Royal Mile from the Castle to the Palace of Holyroodhouse, that historic stage on which so much of Scotland's story was fashioned. They look down, too, on Canongate kirkyard—where lie the remains of Robert Fergusson, poet; of Clarinda, the friend of Robert Burns; Adam Smith, the author of the *Wealth of the Nations*; along with many others who played their prominent part in the intellectual and physical sturt and strife that go to shape a nation and give character to its people.

Hill races take place in many parts of Scotland but the daddy of them all is the annual lung-bursting hurtle from Fort

37

William to the top of Ben Nevis, Britain's highest peak at 4406 feet, and back. Fourteen miles of gruelling effort but the mountain is there to be climbed and, for some, the more exquisite challenge is to take it at the run.

When the call of the nearer hills is answered, new and precious experiences come fast to the man who walks the hills. As legs tune to the strain of lifting his body over rough ground in an ascent of 3000 feet or so, he will revel in a new fitness—a euphoria indeed. He will sense the sharp savour of physical well-being in new material ways which will come to him like a spiritual benison. Lungs which have been expanded to their fullest will feel purified in the clear fresh air where the eyes will see farther into the distance and where the nearer features will become sharper and more colourful.

The Sidlaw Hills were my stamping ground during the long summer holidays of boyhood. That was before our eleven-plus, and our objective at the end of the six-mile walk was the lower slopes and the blaeberries which grew thickly. While we were staining hands, lips, and teeth blue by eating six berries for every one that we put in the can for jam, my eyes kept lifting to the hills. It became important to climb Craig Owl and White Tap to see Strathmore and the Cairngorms to the north.

Let no one scorn the smaller nearer hills. The Sidlaw Hills which run from the mouth of the Tay into the Ochils, into the Campsie Fells and end in the Kilpatrick Hills at the mouth of the Clyde, can test the stoutest legs and lungs. Anyone who has climbed Dumgoyne, that volcanic stob of the western end of the Campsies, knows that it is stiff and steep, but how well worth the effort it is. From the cairn on top can be seen an exhilarating panorama. The whole spread of Glasgow lies to the south. To the north over Menteith lie the hills of the Trossachs, and piled up behind are all the Highland hills stretching beyond the horizon. But to the west is the loveliest view of all. Beyond the lush rolling farms of the Endrick stands shapely Ben Lomond gracefully dominating bonny Loch Lomond and the hills and peaks surrounding it.

Familiarity and proximity to Glasgow make Ben Lomond a target for the trippers and lots of them gaily traipse their way up the path from Rowardennan—a hotel, a youth hostel and a pier are just about all there is to Rowardennan, together with one of the bonniest settings on that bonny loch. But Ben Lomond is 3192 feet high and near the top it is a steep scramble with quite a sharp drop on the north-east face. As any climber knows, arctic conditions can be encountered at almost any time on the Highland hills, and Ben Lomond— familiar though it may be, is a harsh place in mid-winter snow. It is a different hill altogether when it is approached from the Loch Ard side where it is steep and precipitous.

But in the Glasgow area it is known as "The Ben." This rendering of the Gaelic *beinn* or hill is one of the happiest of the anglicisations and tends to draw everyone to its slopes as a friend, and so it is that many a young boy or girl has found there a first introduction to the thrill of conquering a first "Munro." When you climb, Munro is one of the first names that you learn. Sir Hugh T. Munro listed the separate peaks and tops over 3000 feet and came up with a total of some 540 or so. Collecting Munros becomes a sport in itself, for anything that is over 3000 feet can present a permanent challenge or a sudden ferocity if the weather changes without warning. and that goes for friendly Ben Lomond too.

For the most part of the year, however, Ben Lomond is busy with all kinds of ploys going on. I remember one occasion when camping well up the Ben, being wakened just before dawn by a clattering of stones and by voices that were alternately swearing and laughing. We saw the lanterns but decided that the hilarity precluded any emergency. Next morning, we met the young men responsible. They had been climbing to see the sunrise from the top, a favourite pursuit on the Ben. They decided to make a race of it to see if they could get up as fast in the dark as they could in daylight. They did. "Twenty minutes is the time we allow ourselves for each 1000 feet of normal climbing in daylight; that's the time we made in the dark," they told me.

When I was in my late teens, I was fortunate to be engaged in correspondence with Maurice Thiriet who lived near Paris and who became an important composer of music. He came to have a holiday with me and I fitted him out with a kilt. We went walking and camping in the Highlands which were so close to the small town of Bearsden, near Glasgow, where I then lived. Bearsden, although it is a dormitory suburb of Glasgow, is fiercely independent of its larger neighbour and is determined to keep its separate importance. I once sat behind two Bearsden men in the bus from Glasgow and I could not help hearing their exchanges about London and the people they knew there. "Aye," said one of them thoughtfully, "It's a wonderful place London. It absorbs so many folk from Bearsden alone." And that puts both Bearsden and London each in its proper place.

Maurice Thiriet kept picking up wild flowers, asking me their names. He recognised some of them by their French names and their botanical terms. My comparative ignorance shamed me. He awakened me to an awareness of the wild flowers and I owe him an enormous debt. As I was writing these words of tribute I was due to answer a letter from him. My custom was to draft it in French, leave it for a few days, then to polish the grammar and the spelling. I had just posted my letter when I learned to my great sorrow that Maurice Thiriet had died suddenly of a heart attack at the family farmhouse at Puys near Dieppe. Now when I walk a hill, particularly in the wetter west, I see that the hillsward I tread is a kaleidoscope of colour and I thank Maurice Thiriet. I see the white of the eyebright, the blues, pinks and heliotropes of the milkwort, the exotic grace of orchis and of the bog asphodel, and I relish the pleasure. I am aware, now, that on these western Highland hills, the verdure is fragrant with more scents than can be accounted for by the pervasive bog myrtle.

In the late fifties at a historical conference in Linlithgow, I met two nuns from Nova Scotia. One was a MacDonald and a sister of a previous Prime Minister of Nova Scotia. The other was a MacDonell. Although both were generations away from Scotland and spoke with firm Canadian accents, they were still native Gaelic speakers to which they brought an equally firm Canadian accent. They had recently visited what they described as the battlefield of Cullo*h*den. Sister MacDonald told me, "I wanted to bring a sprig of fraoch from the battlefield but there wasn't any (*it was May and the heather was three months away from blooming*). Someone standing by said 'But you must take something back.' He picked a sprig of roid but I wouldn't touch it."

It is a fascinating vignette. Fraoch, or heather, is the badge of the MacDonalds and roid, or bog myrtle, is the badge of the Campbells. Although these two nuns were pledged to a life of charity and forgiveness and although they were generations away from their homeland, along with their language they had retained an awareness of clan history. They remembered what their battlefield acquantance had forgotten—that it is very difficult for a MacDonald to forgive a Campbell.

B* 41

Not far from Ben Lomond is Ben More near Crianlarich. It is a little under 4000 feet and is almost conical. It is a straight slog upwards without respite and, having got to the top, it then becomes important to climb its twin peak of Stobinian. And that is how the fever develops. But another fever is likely to start at that point. Ben More is a big hill and that is precisely how it has been named in Gaelic—Beinn Mor (big hill). When a young climber asks for the first time what a Gaelic place name means, he is hooked. He learns that the names for the most part are topographical descriptions and that even a superficial knowledge of them could be helpful. He learns that Meall is a rounded hill, that Maol is a bald bare hill, that Garbh means rough and that Fada means long. He suddenly becomes aware of a language and a heritage. Some stop at the point of superficial knowledge (which can by itself be satisfying) but others follow the gleam. They acquire a deeper understanding of their country, its language, its history and their forebears; with the developing knowledge of the men they came from they arrive at a better understanding of themselves, and the adventure of physical striving up a hill has led imperceptibly towards the deeper wisdoms.

So far I have been referring to climbing as a method of reaching the tops. There is, however, the tougher and more demanding sport of rock-climbing which generally involves choosing the hardest way up.

Just west of Ben Lomond, there is a group of hills around the head of Loch Long. It includes the celebrated Cobbler on which the young climbers from Glasgow cut their teeth. Here, again, familiarity tends to blur the physical dangers and challenges, but whether it is high summer and the rocks are dry, or mid-winter with snow and ice on treacherous surfaces, the Cobbler is a climb to be respected even although it is only a matter of an hour's run from Glasgow.

Near Ben More there is Cruach Ardrain, again a hill which rock climbers have made their own. Only about two hours from Glasgow or Edinburgh, it is certain to be tough in winter and that is how the climbers like it particularly when they are young and beginning.

Once the aspiring rock climber has learned his basic skills, he has some of the most exhilarating and challenging faces open to him. The Arran peaks have long been noted for their rocks, the Cuillins of Skye have some of the finest hard rock to be found anywhere, and Ben Nevis has the highest mountain precipices in Britain.

As a consequence, we produce some very fine climbers who may not all be world class, although some of them undoubtedly are, but there are a lot of our young men and women from all walks of life and from all parts of the country who spend their week-ends on the hills. They are so much the better for it and they bring to their climbing a democratic Caledonian camaraderie.

In the fifties, four of these climbers decided to mount a Himalayan expedition. They were Tom MacKinnon, Bill Murray, Douglas Scott and Tom Weir. Characteristically they determined that they would not ask for subventions on the spurious excuse of investigating flora and fauna and other specious pursuits. They financed themselves for six months by hard saving and planning. Their story, *The Scottish Himalayan Expedition*, was notable for its verve but, most of all, for the way in which it was made clear that they did not regard the Sherpas as convenient hill ponies. For the first time in such records, the Sherpas emerged as fellow mountaineers. Indeed, Tom MacKinnon—a neighbour of mine at the time and a modest, almost shy, man (although he was then rated one of Britain's foremost alpinists), brought some of the Sherpas, with whom they had climbed, over to Scotland subsequently as his guests and took them climbing in the West Highlands and on the Cuillins in the Isle of Skye. He will, no doubt, squirm to have this told of him but someone has to record it as an example of natural world citizenship brought about by a common heritage in the high hills.

Incidentally, that book was preceded by one by Ben Humble who, although practically stone deaf, is a noted mountaineer and photographer. Ben's book *On Scottish Hills* broke new photographic ground. Until its publication, photographs of mountains had been notable for the studious way in which the photographer set out to exclude all blemishes of human activity. Indeed, at that time, Alastair Dunnett coined a jocular wounding phrase about Bill Thomson who was quite the most assiduous of the photographers in contriving that no one would appear anywhere in his pictures to spoil them. Looking at one of Bill's excellent photographs, Alastair observed to him, "The Highland Clearances, illustrated by William S. Thomson." It was not meant unkindly, for Bill Thomson had pioneered Highland photography with great single-mindedness and a developing technique. As a young bank clerk in a small Glasgow branch office of the then Commercial Bank of Scotland, Bill rigged up the back shop as a dark room. On Mondays, the results of his week-end forays and his busy work in the dark room would appear in the frames where the clients were accustomed to seeing the bank's last balance sheet. As the customers looked at the unfamiliar scenes with puzzlement, Bill would say, "Like it? Sell you a print for half a dollar."

That kind of entrepreneurial effort was not quite what the

Bank wanted to encourage and they suggested to Bill that he ought to consider giving the whole of his time and none of theirs to his hobby. Bill did just that. He went on to become the man who brought colour photography to the Highlands with results that no one has yet bettered. It is a matter of great pleasure to me and to those who knew him to see that the views which Bill Thomson pioneered—on a bicycle—have been made hard-standing viewpoints for motorists in the Highland area. These hard standings are permanent memorials to the man who found them first and who was in every way a character.

Ben Humble's book is in its own way also a landmark. In his photographs of mountains, the mountaineer is featured. His photographs are as much a record of human striving as of the Deity's physical creation. I like to think that the Lord approves the greater emphasis on his greater creation.

A comparatively recent development on the hills has been in the skiing potential of three areas in particular—Glencoe, Glenshee and Cairngorm. A lot of snow falls in Scotland but our western shores are influenced by the Gulf Stream and, in the west, the snow remains wet and soggy and it does not lie for long. In the Central Highlands it is colder and harder. On the northern slopes the snow can lie for a very long time. Indeed, the Munros held their lands in annual rent of a snowball from Ben Wyvis to be paid on demand to the Sovereign in summer. So far, the Munros have never had to default.

When Jock Kerr Hunter, then the senior technical adviser to the Scottish Council of Physical Recreation, tried in the fifties to enlist my interest in his dream of a skiing development, I was sceptical. I did not think that the snow would last long enough or that it would be of good enough quality. I was wrong. On Cairngorm, the skiing development has been successful beyond imagination. New hotels have been built, new houses, new schools, new roads. Speyside is pulsating with new life and vigour. People from the cities have found new and satisfying jobs in that lovely invigorating area. Bob Clyde, a Glasgow engineer, is now the successful manager of the Cairngorm ski undertaking. Frith Finlayson, another Glaswegian, runs a successful ski school and hotel. Their children have grown up in the healthy setting, and have grown up with snow and skis as a birthright. Fraser Clyde is an international skier and Ian Finlayson competed in the 1971 Winter Olympics. For the Bob Clydes and the Frith Finlaysons new horizons were opened up, but for their children there is now scope for endeavour on the world's scene where the next crop of Scottish children of the snow are again competing with their peers.

The skiing story is only beginning. There are other slopes and other areas which are being surveyed and which will attract more people into the farther hills. Ben Wyvis is one such, and it will not be long before it, too, has its devotees finding their way to new and healthy thrills. When that happens, parents must stand back and find fortitude in the thought that it is better for their children to risk life and limb in the clean air of the hills than in other activities in which mind and soul are put at risk. I speak from experience. My own son, who had been on skis for only a few hours and, even then, at intervals of years, announced to his mother, his sister and me on top of Cairngorm, "I'm going down that." "That" was the "White Lady" ski run, rated as very severe. My wife nearly threw a fit so I hustled her and my daughter on to the chairlift out of the way and said to my son, "When you get to the top of the run, if it looks too difficult, take your skis off and come down in the chairlift." I then watched him as he approached the top of White Lady—which must look almost vertical to a beginner. He stopped at the top to pause and analyse the course of events which had brought him to this uncomfortable decision. Then he set off, stemming his way down very carefully. I didn't like it much but I have done some daft things in my day and I felt that he was entitled to his own daring.

From time to time, when climbers get into difficulties, the cry is raised that there should be regulations aimed at preventing their taking of risks beyond their capacity. I can sympathise with the reason for that reaction but I disagree with it. Young men should pitch themselves against challenges with courage and gaiety. Better if they can be taught how to do so safely, but risks cannot be eliminated totally from life. I would rather that our young men dared than that they should be cautious and, in the end, fearful.

More than three hundred years ago, the Marquis of Montrose —the Gallant Marquis of history—expressed it succinctly for all his compatriots:

> He either fears his fate too much
>   Or his deserts are small
> That dares not put it to the touch
>   To gain or lose it all.

CHAPTER THREE

Where the river's dying throws the sea gates wide
lie the thousand islands waking still on Clyde.
Round the isles of Albyn where our singing bides,
aye to nameless music lift the swinging tides.
At the daylight's ebbing, when the tales are told,
dying sun in sea's deep lights our trail of gold.

NOWHERE is the capacity for enjoyment and adventure more richly available than around our fretted coasts. In the west, the sea lochs provide safe, colourful sailing; there is also always a lee shore for shelter.

I was lucky. I learned to row on the Tay at Dundee and I learned to sail on the Clyde. I had had an early baptism in the cold unforgiving North Sea before I savoured the softer seas of the Hebrides and the west.

It is customary nowadays to refer to the bad old days and to the depression years between the wars, but that was not my impression of how we lived. As I say I was lucky; lucky in the sense that my contemporaries, from all their varied backgrounds, were a gay lot. They took life as it was and made their own way and their own enjoyment. When we could afford a train or a bus we took it; if not, we walked and enjoyed the walk the more but we saw what we most wanted to see—our own hills and the seas around us.

Dick Anderson lived in Greenock. He sold his motor bike during the years of depression and bought a yacht. That's right, a yacht. For around £100. A beautiful six-metre. What a time we had in that yacht sailing around the Firth of Clyde and its sea lochs. We had little money but we had freedom and the zest of discovering for ourselves the many lovely rewarding anchorages where, returning at night to the yacht, we rowed back over a mirror-flat phosphorescent sea which our oars splashed into a shimmering silver splendour.

Later, Dick got himself married and changed his yacht to a very comfortable Belfast Lough class which slept four. His wife was marvellous. Dick was still free to ask us for week-ends or longer. The only differences were that there were curtains in the cabin and other similar refinements to the domestic arrangements. It was noteworthy, too, that our plenishing became more prudent. We did not, for instance, bring more food than was needed for the meals. The yacht slept four so there was no nonsense about buying, say, a pound of tomatoes. The order was for four tomatoes. It was an interesting introduction to the severely practical side of femininity—an aspect of life for which most husbands have cause to be grateful.

On one occasion Dick asked me to make up a four for a week which was to include a race to Tarbert, Loch Long. I jumped at it and made arrangements for a week off. There was just one snag. I had developed an abscess in the crook of my right arm and could neither bend the arm nor grip with my right hand. I was due to join the yacht at 4 p.m. on Sunday, and so on Saturday night I took my abscess to my doctor and persuaded him to lance it. On Sunday, with my arm bandaged almost from wrist to shoulder, but at least with the ability to grip and pull a sheet, I set off for Gourock.

When I arrived, the yacht had gone and I assumed that Dick had taken her out for a spin. Indeed, away out in the Firth there was a yacht of a similar rig, but by 6 p.m. it was clear that they had gone off and, by then, the last outgoing steamer had left. I decided that I would spend 24 hours looking for the yacht and then, if I hadn't found her, that I would take the first ship to the islands for a week's walking. The point was where to begin the search. I remembered vaguely that Dick had made mention some weeks before of Tighnabruaich in the Kyles of Bute, but how to get there with the last steamer gone was the problem.

I took the bus to the Cloch Lighthouse and got a small ferry to Dunoon. There I asked a taxi driver what he would want to run me to Tighnabruaich. "Three pounds, two and sixpence," he said, well aware that that was a furtune, "but," he added, "there's a bus over there going on a 'mystery tour' and they'll take you to Strachur on Loch Fyne for two and sixpence."

That bus landed me at Strachur at 9 p.m. on a lovely evening 28 miles from Tighnabruaich and I started walking. No one passed me in either direction on the road. I slept for two hours in the heather until a soft smirr of rain woke me and I started to walk again. I arrived at Tighnabruaich at 9 a.m. on Monday. There was no sign of the yacht. I startled a hotel proprietor by asking for a whisky before breakfast. I needed it. When I explained what I had done and what I was trying to do, the proprietor made no bones about breaking the licensing laws in what he was prepared to regard as an emergency.

One of the characteristics of life on a seaboard is that all craft are observed by someone and I was confident that had the yacht been anywhere in the area it would have been noted. Sure enough, by 10.30 I had learned that it was at Colintraive, some six miles back down the Kyles. There were just two snags. The last inward boat had gone and Colintraive was again about 28 miles by road. I contrived to hire a launch and joined the yacht at Colintraive from the seaward and north side just as they were giving up hope of my coming from the south side. There were profuse apologies and I was excused duties for the rest of the day to allow me to trail my hot feet over the side. Dick had advanced the time of departure but I had not received his message.

I tell this story in some detail because it illustrates so well the opportunities for the fun in individual effort and independence of action which were open then and are as open to-day. And how rewarding this can be.

No one who knows the East Coast and its people can fail to be attracted by both but the whole of the eastern seaboard from the north of Scotland to the south of England is bounded by the North Sea. The western seaboard is different in that it is not bounded by one common sea. On the west the sea is a medley of pathways—each a gateway. Each at one time the road to stark hardihood and to heart-rending beauty. And the gateways have names brimming with promise—the Sound of Islay, the Firth of Lorne, the Sound of Mull, the Sound of Sleat, the Little Minch, the Minch; each a name to tell of the rewards waiting for the man who travels these sea pathways to the end.

As the poet put it in the lines at the head of this chapter, "dying sun in sea's deep lights our trail of gold." The isles of the west have the incomparable advantage of the sun setting in the Atlantic with the long afterglow lifting the islands into translucent splendour to give them an ethereal shimmering beauty. One best understands the captivating charm of the Hebrides after seeing a summer sun reluctant to leave, staying on to throw its last rays over and through each island before it finally sinks below the horizon in a last burst of salute to light up the sea and sky with transcendant colours striking at heart and soul.

One appreciates then why the Gael's heaven of Tir nan Og—the Land of Eternal Youth—is deemed to lie somewhere in that glorious sea of colour where the dying sun records the promised golden delights.

There are many places where such a spectacle can be a constant spiritual experience to give a stound to the receptive heart and each of us will have his own favourite view. Mull, seen from Oban or from the lighthouse at the south end of Lismore, is one such: I recall an evening at anchor in Loch Bracadale on the west coast of Skye with the Cuillins close behind us sharply limned against a luminous sky, and all around us a land and seascape lit, it would seem, from inner beauty and with the colours changing from moment to moment: the islands of Eigg, Rum and Canna seen from the sands of Morar against the setting sun have the same quality of inner light as they seem to lose substance and float lightly above the golden sea; Mary Holden Bird captured the beauty of these islands in their many moods in a series of delicate water colours which are now so much prized that even the prints are difficult to obtain.

It is as much the quality of light and scenic background as Celtic blood in the veins which gives colour to the Highland character. And in each island there awaits for the traveller the deep pleasure of meeting people of character.

Some years ago I came across an Indian silk pedlar who travelled Skye selling his goods at the cottage doors. He conducted his affairs in pidgin Gaelic and answered with delight to the name by which the Sgianachs knew him—Dougal. It was a nickname of delight all round, especially to the Sgianachs who had chosen the name, for Dougal in

Gaelic means "Black stranger." The Race Relations Board to-day might not approve, but Dougal was happy and clearly felt that he had been accepted for himself, as indeed he was.

I often think that our native curiosity about a stranger protects us from serious racial bias. We want to know about him and where he came from. It is an honest interest and we are as quick to tell him about ourselves and the country we live in. An Englishman tends to talk about Englishmen and foreigners. The Scot tends to distinguish and to say Frenchman, German, Spaniard, Greek, Indian, Chinaman, Jew. He tends to be specific and to recognise in each man the separate dignity along with the separate nationality, and as a consequence is less likely to effect a superiority. In passing, it is a matter of record that, unlike most of the other countries of Europe, Scotland at no time persecuted the Jews. One must, however, confess that from time to time we did a thorough job of persecuting ourselves.

At the north end of Mull lies the island's capital of Tobermory, *Tobar Mhuire*—Mary's well. Everyone falls in love with it for its colour, its charm and its people, all 600 of them. It is a popular harbour for yachts, fishing boats and crafts of all kinds either coming in for shelter or getting ready to stick a nose out beyond Bloody Bay and Ardnamurchan. The wide, safe bay is partly locked by the lovely little island of Calve.

When I first knew the island of Calve, it was farmed by the MacDonalds. By twentieth-century standards it was in many ways hideously inconvenient but it had a uniquely idyllic quality. True, the water had to be collected daily from a spring; shopping was conducted by boat, a row of a mile and a quarter each way and, if the weather was rough, it meant rowing across the narrows and a walk of two miles each way; the stock had to be forded on and off the island or transhipped by boat. But the compensations of that simple, stark life were many. The beauty of the setting was superb through all the changes of the year, with a glorious panorama of sea and hill wherever the eye looked—Ben Hiant in Ardnamurchan to the north, Ben More in Mull to the south, and always the lovely, busy little port of Tobermory over the bay. Calum was a big, strong farmer, as vigorous in a boat as he was on the fields or with a cabar, always ready for a ploy whether it was the Highland Games or the Western Isles Regatta; the two girls, Janet and Margaret, started each day with bakings of scones and pancakes respectively. Perhaps what stands out most in my mind is that as long as the MacDonalds farmed the island, the young men and the older men in Tobermory saw, several times a week, one or other of these girls rowing for the family shopping right throughout the year in wild weather equally with the calm. Both girls preferred the often-dangerous struggle with wind and wave to the chore of lugging heavy purchases for two miles on a path round the bay to the narrows. It was a demonstration of adventurous living by two lassies, and a standing challenge to any man who might have been tempted to feel that life was unfair to him. Janet is now a douce housewife in Edinburgh but when she was on Calve her ability to pull a boat in the water or up the jetty was formidable and more than once put me and my masculine pride in muscle to shame.

Before the MacDonalds went to Calve and while they were farming on Mull, Janet was alone in the house one day when the local "daftie" came in, sat down at the table between Janet and the door, put his hands over his face and stared at her through his spread fingers trying to frighten her. He succeeded but, recounting it, Janet said, "I got between him and the felling axe and if he'd come near me I'd have used it."

57

It was and still is a blood-curdling prospect. That daftie would have been split clean in two had he put Janet to the test.

I was sorry when the MacDonalds left Calve and the island went out of daily use. It seemed to me to have a deadening effect on the whole of that corner of Mull. But adventurous living is endemic there and the island is now owned by Mrs Phyl Cotton. Commander Cotton, who was in the Navy, bought the island but died some years ago. Mrs Cotton with great gallantry lives on the island for a large part of the year, frequently on her own for long periods, and is once more demonstrating how a woman of spirit can overcome adversity, and give the men who have the percipience to observe it a lesson in life lived in adventure.

On one occasion when I had arranged to visit the island with my brother, we arrived in Tobermory to find a gale blowing. The trysting place for all who know the area is invariably the Mishnish Hotel on the sea front. I expressed some doubt to Bobbie MacLeod, the proprietor, about Mrs Cotton being able to get off Calve to meet us. "She'll be here," Bobbie declared with conviction, "Nothing stops her." A few moments later he said, "Look, there she is." It was the only boat, large or small, moving in the bay. In due course, Phyl came into the lounge of the Mishnish, soaking, her blonde hair plastered wetly to her brow, and in her bare feet. It was a striking example of determination to maintain control of events and keep to course. I was interested to note then and later how her courage and independence have made an impression on the people in the area, who speak of her life on the island with affection as well as respect.

Although I have visited and stayed on Calve many times I still look back on a Hallowe'en party on the island as perhaps the happiest demonstration of how adventure comes naturally to life in the islands. As the appointed time arrived, we could see boats with storm lanterns aboard being rowed out in the darkness from Tobermory; we could see storm lanterns bobbing along the path above the narrows presaging the "halloos" for ferrying. Few preliminaries to a dance can be half so satisfying or successful as a journey in the dark by rowing boat. That dance was held in the hay loft which had been cleared and decorated. Apart from the risk of dancing over the edge in the exuberance of country dancing there was an additional hazard to be guarded against—the long nails pinning the slates to the roof protruded several inches and there was always the danger of impaling a gay partner. When the dance was over the guests went home by boat or were ferried across the narrows, always accompanied by the ubiquitous storm lanterns.

If anyone reading this begins to think that Calve is among one of the more desirable of the Hebridean islands, I have only this to say. I agree, it is. But if it ever comes on to the market again will you all please stand back—me first.

There is an excellent new car ferry pier at Craignure in Mull. It is there partly because a native of the island—John Cameron —put up some money to encourage the project. John Cameron was at one time the chief executive and shareholder of Binns Stores in Sunderland, Newcastle, Middlesbrough and the north-east of England before they were bought by the House of Fraser. He was an enthusiast for his native tongue and used to have a pocketful of half-sovereigns handy when he walked along the front in Tobermory. He would speak to the children in Gaelic and if they answered him in Gaelic he would give them half a sovereign. If he could come back now I think he would be disappointed at the way the money would remain in his pocket.

There was another John Cameron in Tobermory who was more readily identified by his nickname of Locheil. Indeed his wife was always referred to as *Bean Locheil* (Mrs Locheil). Locheil was a noted strong man in his day and a bit of a humorist, too. He would respond to any challenge. Once, while fencing in Ardnamurchan he was told that another strong man had carried four coils of fencing wire. Locheil got his colleagues to put a coil of wire on each of his arms and two coils over his head. The ground was boggy and the weight drove him down like a paling stob and he couldn't lift his feet. When he was told that the same man in Ardnamurchan had lifted himself off the ground in a barrel, Locheil had to have a go too for the fun of it. He very nearly succeeded.

When Alastair Dunnett and I had our canoes on Calve, Locheil was fascinated by the craft and by our adventure. Incidentally, he was one of the very few who approved of what we were doing and who did not condemn it as foolhardy. As Alastair Dunnett has described it in *Quest by Canoe*, Locheil just had to have a go. We stripped one of the cockpits for him for, by then, he was gnarled and bent and needed room. Off he went, listing alarmingly to starboard to the delighted hysteria of the MacDonalds. Alastair and I were less amused. We felt some responsibility. "Can he swim?" we asked but no one knew and no one seemed to be worrying. Locheil finally splashed his way back and pronounced the canoes safe. "I'd cross the Minch in her myself," he declared in Gaelic, "and nothing in my hand but a spade."

Years later in London I wanted to contact Locheil's son, Ian, who was a sergeant in the police. Outside Madame Tussauds I asked a young constable (it was the appropriate police division) if he could tell me where I could find Sergeant Ian Cameron. No, he didn't know of a Sgt. Ian Cameron. From

Tobermory in Mull, I added. No, he didn't know of anyone from Tobermory. In desperation, I suggested that he might know a Sgt. Ian Locheil. Of course, he said. Yes, everybody knew Ian Locheil. And a Hebridean nickname identified a man in London when the name on his birth certificate drew a blank.

The MacDonalds of Calve were great friends of the Mac-Kinnons who were their nearest neighbours—a mere row across the narrows and a mile walk across a hill path. It was in the MacKinnon's house one Hallowe'en that I first tasted fuarag, a splendid dish of whipped sour cream with toasted oatmeal mixed through it together with a scattering of the Hallowe'en trinkets. Although we supped it in hilarity from a communal bowl, I have never forgotten that first taste of fuarag which seems to me by comparison to make to-day's mass-manufactured yoghourt an insipid dish fit only for the effete.

Willie MacKinnon presides over the bar at the Mishnish Hotel. Get to know him. He can cut your hair, play the fiddle, tell you how to make fuarag, and give you instruction in Gaelic.

There was a time when, if I wanted to go from Glasgow to Oban, I used to contrive it that I could go off on Thursday afternoon. I would go to the Broomielaw and take McCallum Orme's cargo boat, the *S.S. Hebrides*, which was scheduled to sail at 4 p.m. and usually left at 6 p.m. It was only 90 miles from Glasgow to Oban by road but the journey by ship was an idyll. Two hours down the Clyde and I would be ashore at Greenock like a tourist, then it was off down the Firth to round the Mull of Kintyre through the night. At 5 a.m. we would be alongside the pier at Port Askaig in the island of Islay. Jura would be across the sound coming awake in the

61

early morning light. And all around was beauty, clean and fresh. From Islay we steamed at nine or ten knots up through the Garvellochs past the Isle of Mull and into Oban for noon. It was only an overnight journey but it seemed like a week.

One of the personal sagas of the Inner Hebrides concerns Colin Roy of Port Charlotte in the Island of Islay. Colin was a banker who found himself promoted to a London with which he became disenchanted. He asked for a transfer back to Scotland, a request which his boss made clear was tantamount to heresy, since a job in London was the proper objective of every proper young Scot. Colin differed and, eventually, Colin was saying to his manager, "Look. Either you write to head office and ask for my transfer back to Scotland or I will." Well, there was only one consequence to that and Colin one day met it and went to Euston to buy himself a one-way ticket to Glasgow. His people had connections in Islay and Colin went there to try to find his fortune. He took up the agency for Calor gas, he tried to farm lobsters while that was an early vision and he started a hotel. He had a rough time but to-day he and his family have an outfitters' shop, a shoe shop, and a slaughterhouse backed up with a butchery. As a consequence, the people of Islay can buy clothes and shoes which fit them instead of having to buy, hit or miss, by post and they can now buy and eat the meat which they grow themselves instead of having to import inferior beef and mutton. I, for one, take off my hat to Colin and, some day, Islay will acknowledge the sterling job which he has done for them on their behalf.

When McCallum Orme were bought by MacBraynes I got to know Andy Rome of MacBraynes and through him I was put on a very privileged list of passengers who could book on to the MacBrayne's Hebridean cargo boats, the *Loch Ard* and the *Lochcarron*. Each had two double-berth cabins for special passengers and the cabins were always fully booked well ahead. These ships were for the cognoscenti but MacBrayne's normal services from the mainland to the islands have all the colour that the normal traveller wants. Although Robert Louis Stevenson said that "to travel hopefully is better than to arrive," for most of to-day's travellers the destination is more important than the journey. Even so, no matter how MacBraynes contrive to cut their timings, they cannot reduce the scenic content in the background whether it is a journey to the Inner Isles or to the Outer Isles, and even the most blase traveller cannot fail to be captivated. The new and faster ferry services to Islay, to Mull, to Skye, to Lewis and North Uist make it easy to get to whichever island takes your fancy. You can fly to Lewis or to Barra but, unless time presses, the better way to go is by sea. Flying to Barra is a direct hop from Renfrew near Glasgow. Go by sea and you sail from Oban up the Sound of Mull to Tobermory, out to Coll and Tiree and then to Castlebay in Barra; a holiday in itself. If the Minch is kind, it will be for you a passage of scenic beauty in the near view and in the far. If the Minch is not kind, it will be an experience which you can later describe as bracing.

At the beginning of the century, there was a certain amount of heart-burning on the islands of Barra and Vatersay. Barra was beginning to be overcrowded and Vatersay, across the bay, was empty. The crofters of Barra asked the landowner, Lady Gordon Cathcart, if they could be given permission to settle the neighbouring island of Vatersay. The answer was a resounding no. The island, they were told, was unsuitable and it could not support anyone. It was a stupid answer and the people of Barra set out to prove it so. Twelve crofters went to Vatersay and settled on it. That was in 1908, and the

63

law was set in motion to show the crofters that they had no title to live on their own islands.

Well, there are people living on Vatersay to-day and living well. Years later, I had the pleasure of meeting two men who were closely connected with that episode. One was John L. Kinloch who had gone to Oban to give support to the crofters who had been arrested for trespassing. He found the crofters in the jail in Oban sitting in their shirt sleeves along with the police sergeant, also in his shirt sleeves, playing cards as equals. When the Glasgow pressmen were announced, the interview had to be delayed long enough to allow the sergeant to put on his uniform. The other contact was with a prison warder from Loch Liuchart who, as a warder in the Calton Jail, had on his record the only black mark against him in the whole of his prison career; he had been found talking in Gaelic to the Vatersay squatters and passing them tobacco.

It is only a short sail by ferry from Barra to the island of Eriskay—Eriskay of the Love Lilt, of Bonnie Prince Charlie, of its own breed of pony, and of the *S.S. Politician*, the ship which went aground during the war and gave Compton Mackenzie the hilarious background for *Whisky Galore*. Eriskay has a captivating character of its own. It looks different from the other islands, its people seem as different as do its ponies; it has an air that can only be described as fey. The view from the little hill on Eriskay is as memorable as the view from Barra's Heaval but it too is different in a way which makes a peculiar appeal to the heart.

Another ferry will take you north across the sound to Polochar, South Uist, where there is a delightful historic little inn looking out across the Atlantic. From the bar door you could toss a bottle into the Atlantic and, if the wind was right, the first land it would bump into would be America.

In the Hebridean islands they have their own peculiar problems. They have no industries, the population is scattered sparsely throughout the islands, and the centres of administration are separated from them by sea and by time. Naturally, irritations arise out of the feeling of remoteness and the islanders assume, not without cause, that no one cares about them. On one such occasion I was visited at The Scotsman Publications office in Edinburgh by Donnie MacNeill of the Polochar Inn. Donnie and I were old friends and he had a problem he wanted to discuss with me. The B.B.C. signals were too weak to be received acceptably in the Outer Hebrides and he wanted my support for a petition he was organising. He was certain, he said, that he could get everyone in the Outer Hebrides to sign it.

I felt that he was wasting his time and said so. "What I," asked him, "what do you think anyone in London is going to do about a complaint from the Outer Isles signed by a mere 40,000 people whom they would regard as troglodites anyway." I counselled direct action along the lines of Compton Mackenzie's non-payment of road taxes for the island of Barra (subsequently made into the hilarious film *Laxdale Hall*). I suggested that he set up a local committee to run a local radio service and that he should write to the Postmaster General asking for a licence. When the P.M.G. refused, as he was bound to do, the committee should, more in sorrow than in anger, say that they were going ahead to set up the station to provide the service that the BBC had failed to provide, but that they would stop as soon as the BBC produced a better signal. Pye Radio at that time were quoting £500 to put a modest station on the air and I undertook in the meantime to get my London telecommunications colleagues to check on the second-hand market equipment and prices. I was able to tell Donnie that my London colleagues could set him up in business for £100. I also told him that if he set up a company to be called Tir nan Og Radio he could count me in. Well, of course, the reply letter from the P.M.G. was an amused brush-off. So the next step was discussed. This was to say with regret that the committee were going ahead but that they were taking legal advice on claims against both the BBC and the Post Office for fraudulent misrepresentation in charging radio licence fees for a service they had failed to provide, and also to consider the consequent claims for wrongful fines over the years for non-payment of the licences. It could have been as hilarious as *Laxdale Hall*. Unfortunately, however, instead of having a committee of crofters who are notoriously independent, Donnie's committee included people such as teachers who, in the pay of authority, cannot readily set a course of action which would hold authority up to ridicule. It was a happy exercise, however, and no doubt there are other similar areas in which a suitable group could engineer endless amusement for a whole area. It would be easy to provide a local service with a virtually unending series of ceilidhs.

The South Uist school of piping is regarded as one of the finest in Scotland. They have a feeling for pipe music which is strong enough to support any local radio station. They could easily put on a series of piping performances which would keep the whole of the Hebrides and the West Highlands enthralled. It is difficult, perhaps, for the non-Scot to understand how deep the appeal of pipe music can go in Scotland but it is apposite to tell here one story about the late Pipe-major Willie Ross, the senior piper of the British Army and doyen of the Army Piping School based on Edinburgh. Willie was taught piping by his mother in Ross-shire and the story goes

66

that, when Willie was in his heyday as the greatest piper of his time, his mother, listening to his performance, said, "Willie, ye dropped one of your grace notes."

I discussed this project of a local radio station with Bobbie MacLeod, Provost of Tobermory, proprietor of the Mishnish Hotel, former band leader, and a notable performer on the melodeon. He thought it a good idea but didn't like the suggested company name of Radio Tir nan Og. He thought that a local station for his area should be called The Sound of Mull. Brilliant. I hope he sets up a company to run such a station. It would be a popular success. Since Mull is the ancestral island of the Macleans I have told him I will round up enough MacLeans among my acquaintances to put up all the capital he may need.

Let me warn you at this point never to make the mistake of patronising any islander—whether it be on the islands of the west or the northern isles of Orkney and Shetland, they keep themselves abreast of world topics and they have generally thought their way through them to their own vigorous conclusions.

But that in passing, let's get back to South Uist. Father John Morrison was then one of the parish priests. His parish was the one chosen for the controversial rocket range and he was the spokesman for his parishioners whose ground the range was to occupy. It was a famous battle while it lasted and I remember, at one stage, when preparations were at last being made to fire the first rocket, that Father John told me he thought that, as compensation had not yet been agreed, it might be possible to hold up the first firing. I suggested that he ought to poind the first rocket, nail a bill of attachment to it, and have some international fun. His eyes lit up at the prospect but I could see that he had some reservations. The trout were fishing well and every angler will understand what his choice of hobby had to be.

Also in Father John's parish were a series of "fairy houses." These are underground wheel-shaped dwellings linked by narrow underground passages. They were discovered recently when it was noted that the cattle were wary of grazing and walking over some parts of the ground. Investigation indicated that these were areas which were hollow underneath. From the first one to be opened, Fr. John had a cardboard box full of pottery shards and flint arrowheads from which he offered my children their choice. They came away with pottery shards and an arrowhead. Only the Gaelic word *flathail* which in Ireland is pronounced "flahool" can properly describe this cavalier generosity with the stuff of history.

The fords between the islands of South Uist, Benbecula and North Uist have been bridged, and the road and a car are now the link rather than the sea and a boat. And that is a good development which should help to break down barriers and bring about a better understanding of communal interests. One problem in the Hebrides is that the northern islands of Lewis and Harris and North Uist are Wee Free and the southern islands of South Uist, Eriskay and Barra are Catholic, with Benbecula as a kind of no-man's land. But it is a situation which gives rise to a delicious story which can be told in the northern and southern islands with equal acceptance.

The story goes that the man in Benbecula climbed a small hill there one beautiful summer day and, as he stood on the top and gazed on the beauty surrounding him, he lifted up his heart and voice in prayer. "Oh God," he said, "Bless this land. But you can do what you like with Uist."

There are some for whom the seas that lead to the northern isles—the Pentland Firth, the Sounds, the Roosts and the

Voes—have the greater attraction. The Pentland Firth can be rough and unforgiving but it is the pathway first to the Orkneys and then to Shetland—islands where in June the midnight sun stretches fingers of light to bring these golden isles into the fringes of the Arctic's midnight sun.

The Orkneys are as far north as Cape Cod in Greenland and Hudson Bay in Canada and in the north of Shetland you are nearer to Bergen in Norway than to Aberdeen. Great rivers of warm water which start in the Caribbean and stretch out to touch our western coasts and our northern islands give them and us the temperate moderate climate to make life tolerable and the sea swimmable. It is claimed for Orkney that the water can sometimes feel tepid. I cannot say for I have never tested it. I have, however, stripped off in October for a swim in North Bay, Barra, in the Outer Hebrides, had my swim in an Atlantic rippling gently on to the golden sands, and then run myself dry on the sands. It seemed warm enough but I must confess that I prefer the other end of the Gulf Stream where the closer you can get to South America— Grenada for instance—it is a genuinely tepid sea in which one could swim for hours. Regretfully, that claim could not honestly be made for our end—the colder end—of the Gulf Stream.

You will read and you will be told that the Orkneys and Shetland are not Scottish but Norse. That is only half true. The Norse invasions were by longships filled with warriors going viking over sea. They provided fathers for the Orcadians and Shetlanders, but for the most part the mothers were of indigenous stock. Certainly, Orcadians and Shetlanders whom I have met have seemed to have a reasonable complement of Celtic blood and temperament, enough anyway for me to feel readily sib to them.

69

One Orcadian with whom I find an invariable empathy is Harald Leslie, now Lord Birsay, Chairman of the Scottish Land Court. Harald, one of the best-loved men in Scotland, resolutely signs the nationality column in hotel registers as "Orcadian." He is, as a former High Commissioner to the General Assembly of the Church of Scotland, in the Biblical phrase "a man whom the Queen delighteth to honour;" all Scots will know the appositeness of that reference, but for others it should be explained that the High Commissioner is the Monarch's representative and during the Assembly takes up residence in the Palace of Holyroodhouse, there to hold Court.

Harald, a former Q.C. and rarely to be seen other than in his kilt, has a rich resonant voice to which he matches a ready mind and a preference for the vigour of the older tongues. There is a story that, when he was being briefed about a right-of-way case in which gates were being closed at week-ends, the solicitors said amongst themselves that "anyway, this is one time when Harald won't be able to talk about 'the bairns'." They didn't know their man well enough. The case was hardly open when Harald wanted to know, "If these gates are closed, how will the bairns get to Sunday School?"— an essential and basic question from a man whose kindly heart can be most easily stirred on behalf of the young and the under-privileged. And one is left to muse on how much of his temperament derives from the hard Nordic and how much from the softer Celtic. Harald has a home in Edinburgh but he also has one in Orkney, as his Law Lord title of Birsay implies. Incidentally, it is a passion among Scots to ensure that those among us who enjoy temporal preference be assisted to keep their feet on the ground and, when Harald was elevated to the bench and chose the title of Lord Birsay, one of his friends was prompted to bowdlerise a line in Burns to, "Ye see yon Birsay ca'd a Lord." I will not spoil the exquisiteness of the reference by explaining it to those who are unfamiliar with Burns but it is fair to say that, as commentary, it marches nicely with, "Him write a book? I kent his faither." And I can assure you that it is a joke that Harald hugs to himself in Caledonian, or Celtic, or Orcadian, or Norse appreciation.

There is another prominent Scot who domiciles himself in Orkney. Jo Grimond, M.P., might justifiably plead distance and inconvenience. Instead he lives among his constituents with his wife and family, a circumstance which adds considerably to the high general esteem in which he is held in his own country, an esteem which cuts across political borders. Jo, as a concomitant to his political Liberalism, is a strong advocate of devolution in the British Isles. There is no doubt that when national interests and problems are being handled by national assemblies, men like Jo Grimond will bring new vision to match the realisation of the long-cherished dream.

One other Orcadian I must mention, if only for the sake of telling one of his stories, was the late Eric Linklater, author known throughout the literate world. In one of his prefaces, Eric told of the Orkney farmer who was very mean, so mean that he was once seen on his bicycle pedalling furiously to get home in time lest he should be forced to enrich his neighbour's land; a not unimportant point in Orkney which, although about the same size as Midlothian, has more arable land and a formidable reputation for farming efficiency.

One other story from Orkney. There were two bachelor brothers on a croft. One of them became weary of the work, walked out without a word, went to Canada and worked for the Hudson Bay Company for ten years or so until he became weary of that work. He went home to the croft and as he

71

walked through the door his brother asked, "Where have you been all this time?" "Oot," he replied.

It could be the wry, dour, humourously-ironical answer that would be heard in many corners of mainland Scotland.

It is fascinating that the fiddle, which used to be the most popular instrument in Scotland before religious fanaticism frowned on simple enjoyment, is still the popular instrument in the northern isles where in Shetland they can gather together a celebrated group of forty fiddlers who meet to make and enjoy together their own music most of which, by the way, seems to be in the Scottish and not in the Norse idiom.

In addition to its fiddlers, Shetland has its knitters. They produce some of the most delicate of lace knitting in wool but they are best known for their pullovers, jumpers and cardigans in Fair Isle wool in shades varying from light fawn to dark brown knitted into the characteristic patterns. The soft silky wool is plucked or "roo'd" from the sheep and sorted out into its natural colours which give to the garment a delicacy of tone that would be hard to achieve by dyeing.

There is one major irritation involving Orkney and Shetland and it is no fault of the Orcadians or Shetlanders.

The mapmakers, with an understandable urge to economise on paper, will keep looking at the empty printing space in the Moray Firth and will keep inserting the two island groups into the Moray Firth. It is no doubt a convenience in printing but it is a monumental inconvenience in administration. Anyone outside of Scotland would be incredulous at the many instances in which administrators, looking at the map, have lumped Orkney and Shetland with the mainland counties. Not so long ago the islanders were in a fury because some genius had decreed that the fire-fighting services would be administered from Caithness. A fresh look at the map with the islands in their correct geographical relationship would stop a lot of the confusion.

Over the years, I have tried to persuade the Scottish Tourist Board and others always in any illustration to show the islands in their correct geographical relationship. When matters have been under my own control I have always insisted on and have achieved, to my own eye at least, this much more pleasing and decorative pattern.

This chapter was to be about the seas at our door but I see now that it is mostly about people. Well, I did say at the outset that the seas around us were gateways and pathways to the islands. More than half the pleasure to be derived from sailing the seas is to be found in the people who will be encountered at every stage of the way. And wasn't it Alexander Pope who said that the proper study of mankind is man?

CHAPTER FOUR

All rivers run to the sea,
but the sea is not full;
To the place where the rivers flow
there they flow again.

THERE are two Royal rivers, one historic and one comparatively recently come to royal patronage. The Forth and the Dee.

The Forth, which starts at the Highland Line and ends in the North Sea near the Bass Rock and which divides Fife from the Lothians or is the link, depending on how you view running water, has a long royal tradition. It was in Fife that Princess Margaret, fleeing from William the Conqueror, was wrecked. It was she who subsequently married Malcolm Canmore and either put Christianity on the right road in Scotland or distorted it—again depending on your point of view. It is a fact, however, that Queen Margaret's Chapel in Edinburgh Castle was built for her and is the oldest building in that majestic and historic group of buildings surveying the changing city from atop their volcanic rock. A pleasing provision is that any Margaret in Scotland can arrange to be married in Queen Margaret's Chapel. For the monarchy in Scotland there were two places of personal importance to them down the centuries—Edinburgh with its Castle and Seat of Government and Dunfermline in Fife with its abbey and the royal palace at Falkland. As a consequence, the much-used royal route across the Forth took its name from the traffic and the terminals are North and South Queensferry. Dunfermline Abbey holds the body of King Robert the Bruce, and the sculptor Pilkington Jackson was once given the opportunity of examining and measuring the royal skull. From these measurements and with a sculptor's eye for flesh on bone he produced the massive equestrian statue of The Bruce which now stands regally commanding the field of Bannockburn.

One recent North Queensferry man with an inventive turn of mind was the late John Marshall. He worked out an idea for improving dramatically the quality of the sheds which are so much a part of farming life. Using whindust from the local quarry, cement and wire netting, he was in the business of converting draughty sheds into comfortable quarters for stock, or useful working premises for all kinds of jobs. He had converted his own sheds in this way into workshops with lathes and wood-turning machinery using as raw material the teak and other wood from the ship-breakers at Inverkeithing. He also had an association with the local linen factory. He decided, that if he laminated two sheets of linen with latex, he would have a tough waterproof canvas, and that if he linked the canvas to his wood output he could produce a boat. He tried various shapes and then came up with a kayak which he called the Lochaber. Believe it or not, he studied battleship hull design and based the waterline of his canoe on a battleship's line. He tested his canoes in the Forth near the famed railway bridge in rough conditions and then modified his shape to include a hard chine for stability. He fitted one canoe up with a box kite but did not pursue that interesting line when he found that the high winds took charge and that he had no control over where the kite took the canoe.

He made good safe sturdy sea canoes at the time when canoeing was enjoying a resurge of interest. I know how safe and sturdy they were in rough seas. It was in his kind of canoe that I did my own journeyings in the Hebrides.

The other royal river is, of course, the Dee but it is an upstart compared with the Forth and that river's venerable royal connections. Queen Victoria put the recent stamp of of approval on the Dee when she purchased Balmoral and made it the royal holiday home in the Highlands. But the Dee always had a regal setting and the people who live along its banks from Aberdeen to Braemar have never been in any doubt about it. That, indeed, is the chief characteristic of the Deesiders; they have no time for doubt. When they have made up their minds, no power on earth will shift them, and the Lord himself would have a hard time of it trying to convince an Aberdonian that he was wrong. It is in that airt that they tell two apposite stories. One is of the Presbyterian minister who, seeing one of his congregation working openly in the garden on Sunday, dropped a gentle reminder by saying, "The Lord is a wonderful husbandman, John." And John replied, "Aye, minister, but ye should have seen this gairden when he had it a' tae himsel'." The other story is in the sterner uncompromising setting of the Wee Frees where they believe in calling a Sunday spade a tool of the Devil. It was a similar kind of occasion when the Wee Free minister learned that one of his congregation had so far forgotten himself as to dig up a shaw of potatoes on the Sabbath for the dinner. So on Monday, the minister sought out the backslider to upbraid him for his wanton conduct, and was astounded when the offender showed no contrition. "After all, minister," said the offender in his defence, "Christ himself plucked the ears of corn on the Sabbath." "Maybe sae," retorted the outraged minister, "maybe sae. But in this kirk we dinna think ony the mair o' him for 't."

It scarcely matters when the Dee is visited throughout the year. Deeside is always a pleasing prospect. Although it is gorgeous in autumn and majestic in winter, my own preference is for the spring when there is a crispness in the air, the sky is clear, and all around there is the fresh promise of new growth among the grasses, the heathers, the bushes and the silver birches. At that time my heart can be lost to the upper reaches.

The Dee is salmon river all along its length, and a river where, near the centre of the city of Aberdeen, you will see citizens out with rods in the river while the traffic tide of a busy city flows unendingly past them on the road nearby.

There is another traffic tide at the mouth of the Dee where Aberdeen has become one of the principal mainland terminals for the North Sea oil operation. Business is roaring along almost with the inexorable power of a tide rip, and Aberdeen has seen property values soar to fantastic prices. There will be changes as a consequence of the oil development and the influx of new people from different countries and with different ways. I would not like, however, to assume that it will be Aberdeen or the Aberdonians who will change most. The Aberdonians have been around, they have seen much of the world, and they prefer Aberdeen to anything they have seen. As I said before, the Aberdonian is a man of some decision. I have a hunch that, in a year or two, oilmen's families in the United States and elsewhere are going to be a little taken aback when their nearest and dearest returns to the family bosom from his stint among the uncouth natives of North Scotland bearing boxes of finnan haddie, shortbread and bottles of malt, and greets them with, "Fit like? Fu's a' wi' ye?"

You see, in Aberdeenshire they relate all information to the fount of all knowledge which, naturally, is Aberdeenshire. There is the story of the Gordon Highlander who had been stationed in the Middle East and who was home on leave. He was asked where he was stationed and his answer was, "Weel, it's a wee place ye widna richt ken but tae lat ye understaun it's twal' mile on the Achnagatt side o' Jerusalem."

There you have it, then. Precision and decision, the two qualities you will find among the people who live in the lovely country around the Dee.

The river Tay takes its outlet from Loch Tay and flows through some of the bonniest parts of Perthshire before it slides smoothly between Fife and Angus to reach the sea beyond Carnoustie where the bar of the river is a physical phenomenon which can be seen. Up at Grandtully there are a series of cataracts where the canoeists hold their slalom contests in what used to be called white-water canoeing. These contests, which involve going through a series of "gates" (posts hung on wires over the river) and, at times, going back up through them against the cataract flow, also involve the ability to be able to execute an Eskimo roll in the turbulence, for one thing, at least, is certain; someone will inevitably coup his canoe and survival may depend on a skill learned from the Eskimo. Slaloms in the spring are conducted over a cold grey mass of swollen water melting from the snow on the hill. You will hear people look at the river and refer to it as "snaw bree" and that is a precise description of the icy water produced from the melting snows.

By contrast, I can recommend a visit to the Dunkeld House Hotel, a former, grand, shooting lodge down below the road on a placid stretch of the Tay. The hotel is excellently run and is in a splendid setting. If you want, you can arrange to try for a salmon a hundred yards from the hotel itself. Salmon is, of course, a key word all along the Tay. On the upper reaches, you will see rods out. Where the river passes through the city of Perth, you will see rods out. Below Perth you will see salmon cobles on the banks or out in the river for, there, the salmon fishing is not a sport but a livelihood.

You may also see pearl fishing in progress. Tay pearls have a long history. They are represented in the Scottish Royal Regalia. You will find them on sale in the Perth jewellers. You might even get a chance to have a go at finding one for yourself.

The Tay at Dundee is where the whaling fleets used to sail from. To-day it is still the port to which the raw jute is brought to serve the factories, for Dundee is still the jute manufacturing centre of the country. Dundee's world-wide trade has also made it one of the very wealthy financial centres controlling a world-wide span of investments. Dundee does not shout about that but goes about its financial business quietly and very effectively. And, of course, Dundee is the home of the newspaper and magazine publishers known simply as D. C. Thomson, the name of the formidable man who gave to his business a reputation for training, for journalistic and marketing expertise, and for hard-headed anti-union attitudes. D. C. Thomson was very angry when the General Strike stopped his publications in 1926 and from that time on he refused to recognise unions—a policy which his successors are continuing. The operation of the Industrial Relations legislation will compel a change of attitude but it will be a great loss to journalism if anything is allowed to reduce the effectiveness of the D. C. Thomson autocratic method of training young journalists to become the best all-rounders in the industry. There is no namby-pamby concession to the

82

fashion of consultation; the young would-be journalist is told where to go and is told what to do; he also has the inestimable advantage that he is told how to do each job by men who are among the best analysts in the world of how to appeal effectively in simple and direct language to the average reader's instinctive response to human interest.

Arbroath is just past the mouth of the Tay but having written of the salmon in the river it is apposite to refer to the fish which Arbroath has made its own; the smokie. The phrase "Arbroath smoked haddock" is now taken to mean any haddock smoked but how unfair that is to Arbroath and to any connoisseur of food. Most of the "Arbroath" smokies you see on sale will have been trawl-caught haddocks kept in ice until the catch is landed and then smoked, not in Arbroath, having been out of the water for some days. But the real thing is different. And you can see why it is different when you go to Arbroath. The harbour is filled with the wee boats of the line fishermen who catch the haddock at night and whose wives smoke them first thing in the morning. All along the roads around the shore in Arbroath you will see houses with notices advising you that they have smokies for sale. At the back of the houses are the little smoking sheds and huts where a man's catch is metamorphosed by his family into the finest, most succulent table fish ever produced by the effort of man and the wit of woman. You can test the freshness of the Arbroath smokie quite simply by turning back the skin which ought to peel from the flesh. The "Arbroath-type" smokie, on the other hand, has been out of the water so long that its skin is glued on.

To prepare a smokie for the table is simplicity itself. It has already been cleaned and all you need to do is put it in a pan of water and bring it to the boil. Drain the smokie, open it up and remove the bone, which comes out easily. Put a piece of salt butter on the open fish, push it under the grill until the butter melts—and then eat your way to paradise. The only variation to this menu which I would recommend is that, instead of one smokie, you might make it two, or three, or four.

Discussing the relative merits of fresh kippers and fresh smokies in a west coast kippering factory with a herring fisherman, we agreed that the smokie had it by a wide margin. The herring fisherman summed it up in a memorable phrase, "Smokies," he declared, "are bad tae beat. Bad tae beat." I present you with the phrase which, I am sure, you will want to use when you have enjoyed the blessing of your first genuine Arbroath smokie.

I am biased, of course. I was brought up on smokies sold round the doors in Dundee by sonsy Arbroath fishwives from their creels. They were dressed in the traditional fish-wife's outfit of blouse, dark skirt and striped aprons. They generally had two creels, one smaller than the other and the smaller one sat inside the bigger. When the creels were full it took two strong men to heave them up on to the backs of these strapping women. I marvelled then, and still do, at the weights they were able to shoulder from door to door. Having now declared my interest, I will still stand to my claim that there is no fish anywhere to compare with a fresh smokie from Arbroath. It is, indeed, bad to beat. And if you know of a better, I'd be glad to hear of it.

That noble swift river, the Spey, which runs from Laggan in Inverness-shire north through the Laigh O' Moray into the Moray Firth at Buckie, is now becoming namely for winter skiing and for the rapidly expanding holiday centre at Aviemore. It is only a few years since the first concerted development of skiing on Cairngorm was begun, and now in the main street in the little township of Aviemore there are traffic lights to control the flow in and out of the holiday centre.

But the Spey has other reputations. Salmon, of course, are there to be fished but it is around the lower Spey that the key reputation was earned. There, from Glenlivet by the side of Ben Rinnes almost down to the mouth of the river are the little streams draining off the hills to be captured and transmogrified into a succession of malt whiskies of superlative quality. No two of them are alike; not even those produced from two streams from the same piece of hill, each with a bouquet and flavour unique, separate and enticing. Some men will swear by one malt and some by another but more are thirled to the Spey malts than to any of the others whether from Orkney, Islay, Perthshire, Fife or Dunbartonshire—good though they all may be.

At Buckie, at the mouth of the Spey, and to the east along the Moray Firth in a string of little fishing towns you can meet a grand breed of men—the fishermen of the Moray Firth. They can be seen from time to time in their sturdy drifters all round the British Isles where there are herring to be harvested. But this is where they live in these trim little towns with their sturdy houses set foursquare to the weather, all of the houses painted with the same care and devotion that goes to the painting of their ships.

If you have children north with you and want a bit of unusual fun, take them to the Kildonan river in Sutherland and try panning for gold. At one time there was a bit of a gold rush to Kildonan and the local proprietor issued prospecting licences. Nowadays you do not need the licence and the presumption is that you are unlikely to strike it lucky. But

85

you could try. Gold was got there once and it is a sporting chance that gold can still be found. In any case, what an adventure for children it could be. For that matter, when you are hearing tales of glamorous holidays in the Mediterranean, the Canaries, the Indian Ocean, the Caribbean and all the rest of the exotic fashionable holiday haunts, think what a conversation stopper it would be to say, "When I was panning for gold at Kildonan. . . ."

Among all our great rivers there is one of the small ones which will always be revered. It is the Nith, which flows into the Solway through Dumfries. By its banks Robert Burns composed many of his songs and poems. His wife, Jean Armour, told of how he wrestled with the making of Tam O'Shanter as he walked along the banks of the Nith, his mind busy. He passed his wife and children without seeing them, his brow flushed and his eyes shining. "I wish," said Jean, "you had seen him. He was in such ecstasy that the tears were hopping down his cheeks." He was at that moment a man burning with the divine fire, a man touched by the finger of God. He had linked great imagination and high passion to a command of words, words that galloped and charged along.

If for nothing else, the Nith will be namely as the scene for that high adventure of the mind by Scotland's poet. Fame enough, indeed.

Of all our rivers, the Clyde is the best known. It flows through Lanarkshire past farms and orchards until it reaches Glasgow where it becomes an industrial river for twenty miles before it debouches into that glorious estuary, the Firth of Clyde. In the small towns above Glasgow there are memorials to Sir William Wallace. Although he was born at Elderslie on the lower Clyde and educated in Dundee, it was in Lanarkshire that his early exploits took place and it was these which set the country alight and which still fire the young Scot to-day. The first major castle he freed was Dumbarton Castle on the lower Clyde and the first anyone knew of it was when the Earl of Lennox, riding with his followers through Dumbarton, saw the Scottish flag flying over the Castle and went to see what had happened. It must have been quite a moment. The 19th and 20th century story of the Clyde is of industrial and inventive ferment. The building of ships was a proud story until recently and no doubt it will be proud again. The *Cutty Sark*, one of the finest, fastest square-rigged ships ever to dance the waves, was built at Dumbarton. Since then there has been a long line of great ships culminating latterly in the two Queens. During the war, virtually every dirty little patch of mud along the river from Glasgow had some small craft being hammered and welded to keep our country in the fight at sea for survival. On the Clyde many of the war-time convoys and invasion fleets were gathered, and from the Clyde they sailed on their hazardous missions. It was a period of intense activity and high production.

Recently shipbuilding on the upper Clyde has not had such a happy story but the background of tradition, of skill, of craft in building ships is still there and it will show, for the Clyde is the kind of river where one of the memorials on its banks is an early steamship engine. It is also the river where down below Bowling there is a memorial to Henry Bell and his *Comet*, the early steamship from which it all began.

There are on the Clyde, as there have been for many generations, an indigenous craft skill, a commercial vigour and an inventive genius. These qualities may be obscured from time to time but they will never be dormant. There is a bustling quality of all of Clydeside proclaiming that here is a river which nurses a lively, alert and friendly people. Let me at this point go back to the poet whose rowing song of the Clyde, his Clyde Iorrum, heads chapter three:

Iorrum of the river, iorrum of the tide
    Time nor tide shall fear as on the seas of Clyde.
Heroes made our story, stories still shall be,
    And the least shall praise him, Clyde that serves the sea.

CHAPTER FIVE

Bonny waters by the sea,
Bonny hills with lochs of glee,
Bonnier sights there canna be
Than the lochs of Albyn.

ONE of the great boons conferred by a mountainous country is that a lot of water collects in the hollows to provide a pleasant change for the eye and, at the same time, a vast range of activities both for the leisurely-minded and for the energetic. Some of these stretches of water are mere dubs, others are noble lochs held in a frame of majestic hills.

Loch Lomond, a mere twenty miles from Glasgow, could become commonplace because of proximity and familarity but its size, its splendour, save it. Loch Lomond will always be the loch of song and story. The bonny, bonny banks are not just a phrase to match the music of the song; the banks are indeed bonny and at times can take on a transcendent breathtaking beauty. The soft air, the mellow outlines of the hills, the green tree-clad islands or the shimmering loveliness when the sun shines bright on Loch Lomond can be matched only by the same scene when in purple hue the Highland hills we view, and the moon coming up in the gloaming.

It would take a lot of use, indeed it would need a lot of misuse to spoil Loch Lomond. We are fortunate in that the local authorities, the various recreational bodies, and public opinion are sufficiently vigilant to ensure that the development of Loch Lomond as an incomparable playground will not be allowed to destroy the qualities which attract people to it. It is also true to say that there is a high standard of self-discipline exercised by those who have been using the loch for a long time. The Camping Club of Great Britain have had a camp site at Millarochy Bay for many years. As neighbours they have the Clyde Canoe Club. At Rowardennan, the Scottish Youth Hostel Association have an excellent and popular hostel which is also a centre for canoeing. All of these bodies set high standards which their members impose on themselves.

The Clyde Canoe Club is now a venerable organisation. The craft they use on Loch Lomond are sailing canoes which are more like small yachts for size and accommodation. Before the turn of the century one of their members, using a Rob Roy canoe, went round the Mull of Kintyre. The Mull can be a relatively quiet place but it can more often be a fearsome meeting of clashing tidal currents. I used to note how on the *S.S. Hebrides* both on the outward passage and on the inner, there was evident relief on the faces of the crews when we had safely rounded the Mull in bad weather. When the Clyde Canoe Club member went round in on his own, sea-going yachts were sheltering in Campbelltown Loch. One story was that he wouldn't have started if it hadn't been for a bottle of whisky but whether that was true or a joke, nothing should be allowed to denigrate the memory or the courage of that journey. It was about the same time that members of the club made a crossing from Skye to the Outer Hebrides. The canoes they were using were of the same style as those used by Robert Louis Stevenson and of which he wrote in *Inland Voyage*. There was quite a vogue for canoeing at that time. The canoes were modelled on the Eskimo kayak and were pioneered by a John MacGregor whose nickname of Rob Roy was used to describe his design. At one time a member of the Clyde Canoe Club had one of these old timber canoes. It was clinker-built and heavy but had pleasing lines. He put it into Loch Lomond so that I could sit in that piece of history but it was bone-dry, the timbers had shrunk and it leaked like the proverbial sieve. It would have taken a lot of soaking to get it water-tight again.

The canoes used by to-day's experts and which can be seen at the canoeing functions on the loch and elsewhere are slim, short light craft in fibre glass. They are the canoes for slalom competition in the rapids at Grandtully on the River Tay. They have the merit that they lend themselves to the Eskimo roll by which the canoeist can right himself, and also to quick repairs should they be holed.

At Balmaha, there are boats to be hired from Alec Mac-Farlane. My preference was always for a rowing boat. Into it would go the rucksacks and we would be off for a carefree week-end camping for the night on one of the islands. If Alec MacFarlane had known the capers we got up to he might not always have been so friendly and helpful. It was so tempting on a summer day away out on the loch, drifting happily in the sun, to dip a billy can over the side and set it to boil on the Primus stove. That was reckless enough but we generally stripped off then and dived overboard for a swim while the stove roared away in the empty boat. Getting back in again called for care and balance and we did not at any time set fire to a boat, nor, indeed, did we ever knock over the stove. It was a daft caper, nonetheless, and that as well as some other mad adventures tend to make me tolerant of risk-taking by healthy young men.

The daftest ploy on one occasion was to take a sailing dinghy from Balmaha to Balloch on a very rough day. It wasn't a very good dinghy and the pull of the mast had started to spring the timbers. It looked none too safe and then some-one said, "Tie it up like a parcel." That seemed like a brilliant comedy suggestion so everyone piled into scrounging any spare rope and tying the dinghy from end to end and round about just like a parcel. A celebrated Glasgow character known as Puddock Wright, who was no slough himself at mad ploys, watched the preparations thoughtfully but refrained from comment, controlling himself to say quietly, "I hope you fellows can swim." It was a hilarious hysterical passage to Balloch. My task was to accompany the dinghy in my canoe and be ready to help if they landed in the drink. It was an illusory rescue provision. The short steep seas would have made a rescue operation difficult if not impossible. As I say, these capers make me tolerant of wild adventures by others.

Across the loch from Ben Lomond is the Loch Sloy power station. Loch Sloy is up in the hills above Loch Lomond and is in Clan MacFarlane territory. The slogan of the clan is "Loch Sloy." The moon, by the way, is known in that area as MacFarlane's Lantern, a name which tells you all you need to know of the traditional night marauding reputation of the clan.

The Loch Sloy hydro-electric power station was the start of another tradition. It was the first major undertaking by the North of Scotland Hydro-Electric Board and was opened in 1950 by Queen Elizabeth, now the Queen Mother. By now many of the Highland lochs have been harnessed and the power stations, which were carefully designed and sited to harmonise with the landscape and which were in some cases tucked away from the road, have now mellowed smoothly into their settings.

The story of the Hydro Board is an adventure by itself and the story of a man who made his visions come true.

The late Tom Johnston was a determined man—he knew what he wanted. He was appointed Secretary of State for Scotland in the war-time Coalition Government. Winston Churchill, the Prime Minister, thought highly of him and offered him more senior Cabinet posts but Tom Johnston always refused. He had the only job he wanted. He was Scotland's spokesman and he set about using all he had learned in a life-time of politics to get the progress he wanted for his own country. He set up what he chose to call his "Council of State" which was composed of the previous ex-Secretaries of State for Scotland. Together they represented Socialist, Tory and Liberal outlook at a senior political level. His briefing to his Council of State was a model. They were, he told them, to forget the five per cent of things on which they disagreed and were to concentrate on the 95 per cent where they were in agreement. Tom Johnston wanted action and he got it. When he went to the Prime Minister with a proposal on which he wanted Churchill's support, he was able to say "and my Council of State agree." His Council had no constitutional authority but Churchill knew that what Johnston was saying to him was "and I have the people who can unite Scottish public opinion behind me." It was a sound piece of politicking and it brought quick results. In 1943, both Houses of Parliament, for the first time in a century, accepted without a division a major measure for Scotland, and passed the Hydro-Electric Development (Scotland) Act which established the Hydro-Board. Before the war was over, Mrs Johnston was on a bulldozer cutting the first sod 12 feet wide by 100 feet long.

Tom Johnston became the Hydro Board's first chairman

and used every power he had to speed the creation of natural assets and wealth in his own country. He insisted that architects plan good housing in pleasing groups for the permanent staffs who would run the power stations when the thousands of construction workers had moved on to other projects. At a time when brick with an outer plaster cast had universal acceptance, he brought stone masons back into the scene to build the houses as well as the stations in the local stone. The building of dams and the other civil engineering played havoc with the local roads and that suited him. It gave him the excuse to rebuilt and re-engineer the roads to a width and a standard better than before. To enable him to do this he had had included a social responsibility clause in the Hydro Bill.

At that time, he was also Chairman of The Forestry Commission and was looking for a quick way of getting houses into Highland areas in order to get on with the enormous job of planting to make good the inroads and neglect of the war years. He heard that there were service huts of good quality in Cumberland from which the armed services had melted away on demobilisation. He wrote to the Services department involved, who referred him to the Ministry of Works. He wrote to the Ministry of Works and was referred back to the services department. When he saw that he was being given a civil-service run around, he dropped the correspondence. He called in a major contractor and told the contractor that he wanted to borrow the contractor's best clerk of works. He then sent the clerk of works to Cumberland with a fleet of lorries to bring back the huts and to account in triplicate for every nut, bolt and screw. Then he wrote to the Ministry of Works telling them that he had taken the huts and enclosed a copy of the inventory so that they could

96

send him the account for what he had taken. If they wanted to take any other action, he added, his legal adviser was the Solicitor-General for Scotland. Talking about it afterwards he said, "We put the architects of the Department of Health on to these huts and we were able to give the forestry workers the key of the door at a cost of around £560 a house."

He was quite a man, Tom Johnston, and for him I may be permitted to borrow Christopher Wren's epitaph, "If you want to see his memorial, look around you." It is there in the Highlands in houses, roads and hydro-electric undertakings.

Not far from Loch Lomond in the Trossachs you can go and look at Loch Katrine; you can go for a trip in the little pleasure steamer but that is all. You may not use the loch in any other way. It is Glasgow's domestic water supply and they are very proud of it and guard it jealously. But there is plenty of fishing to be had in lochs nearby.

Lovely Loch Lubnaig is one such and is just up the road from the Trossachs through the Pass of Leny.

Beyond Strathyre is Balquhidder—the entry, too often by-passed to-day by the motorist hurrying north, to the two lovely lochs of Loch Voil and Loch Doine set in an area of tranquillity and serenity. But it was not always so peaceful or serene. This is the area where the MacLarens and the MacGregors feuded. In the little church at Balquhidder is the grave of Rob Roy MacGregor, freebooter, cattle rustler, rent lifter, and the man who did more than anyone else to add the word "blackmail" to the language. In that little graveyard there are two other stones, each with long inscriptions, which you have only to read to get a picture of an impassioned sculptor chiselling away in a fury. One is a literary attack on the pedants who have so corrupted speech and spelling that there are people going about saying MacLaren and spelling the clan name that way when everyone ought to know that the descent is from Laurence and that the name ought to be spelt and pronounced MacLaurin. The other records the story of some MacLarens who were "feloniously extirpated by a group of marauding banditti from Loch Tay." Balquhidder is worth the visit if for no purpose other than to be amused by the outspoken vigour of these two tombstones.

By the way, do not imagine that historical passions are necessarily abated. Robin Og, the youngest son of Rob Roy, shot and killed a John MacLaren. By some accounts, Robin Og was regarded as a reasonably good-looking young man but in her history of Clan MacLaren, published in 1970, Margaret MacLaren of MacLaren quotes an advertisement in the *Caledonian Mercury*:

That John MacLaren of Beanchon, in Balquhidder, Perthshire, vassal to His Grace the Duke of Atholl, was on the 4th instant barbariously murdered by Robert Drummond (alias Macgregor), commonly called Robin Oig, son of the deceased Rob Roy MacGregor, by a shot from a gun as he was ploughing, without the least provocation, whereof he instantly died; thereafter he and others, his accomplices, went to the town of Invernenty, and houghed, mangled and destroyed 36 stots and a cow belonging to Malcolm and Donald MacLaren, drovers. Therefore whoever shall apprehend the said Robert, so as he may be brought to trial, shall have 20 guineas reward from James Muirhead, at his coffee-house. He is a tall lad, aged about 20, thin, pale-coloured, squint-eyed, brown hair, pock-pitted, ill-legged, in-kneed, and broadfooted.

Margaret MacLaren is the widow of the late Donald, a colourful character who succeeded in establishing his claim to be chief of his clan. It was always a pleasure to meet him and hear his latest ploy and plans for his ancestral glen. He had, moreover, one quality which singled him out from all the other clan chiefs I have met or heard. He was the only one whose voice and accent were Scottish, a fact which reminded me of Dr Johnson's comment on the sons of the clan chiefs in the late 18th century, that they would be tamed into insignificance by an English education; a sweeping generalisation and they are not all insignificant but there was no doubting the significance of Donald MacLaren of MacLaren or his authenticity.

Not far north of Balquhidder is Loch Earn, where there is a thriving water skiing development centred on the Lochearnhead Hotel and its hefty Highland Games athlete proprietor Ewen Cameron.

When I first knew the Lochearnhead Hotel it was a douce quiet Highland hotel and when I reached it, summer or winter, I used to feel that I was far away from cities and their influence. To-day Lochearnhead is still a well-run Highland hotel with an excellent table but it is a busy place and cheery with water skiers. It is now doing the equivalent of a town trade.

Loch Earn to-day is well used for sport and at the St Fillan's end under the bulk of Ben Vorlich there is a lot of yachting going on. Incidentally, Queen Wilhelmina of the Netherlands used to holiday regularly at St Fillans. When you stand outside of the hotel or walk along the roads which run along each side of Loch Earn you can understand why the Queen from Holland was so attracted to a gentle mountain setting.

Loch Tay from Killin to Kenmore is as glorious a portion of Perthshire as is to be seen anywhere, dominated to the north by the great mass of Ben Lawers from whose peak I saw in the same day a pair of golden eagles, the spire of

Glasgow University and the peak of Goatfell in Arran. The steamer which used to serve Loch Tay was withdrawn a number of years ago but here, as with the sea lochs of the Clyde estuary, is an opportunity to redevelop in terms and methods suitable for to-day a ship service which by itself adds colour and attractiveness to any large sheet of water. Nothing makes any landscape come alive quite so much as to see boats, or yachts or ships moving about their business or their pleasure and for that matter, the loch itself need not be all that big.

Our best known loch is probably Loch Ness in the Great Glen running from Fort Augustus to Inverness. It has its own majesty but I must confess that it is not one of my favourite lochs, despite the intriguing stories about Nessie the Monster. The existence of Nessie is still open to proof and to doubt but those who think they have seen the monster are in no doubt. The monks at the Abbey School, Fort Augustus, have useful brochures about the Great Glen and about Loch Ness and Nessie. Some years ago, a man I knew mounted an elaborate personal expedition to spot Nessie. He patrolled the loch each day and night and was eventually convinced that, not only had he seen Nessie, but that there was an eerie quality about his night encounter which frightened him. What he saw or felt I do not know but he had the wind up and there was no doubt that he certainly believes in the existence of Nessie.

There are boats to be hired in which one can have a splendid holiday with perhaps a chance to see the monster. It is possible then to go from Inverness via Loch Ness, Loch Oich and Loch Lochy to Fort William. The Scottish Tourist Board can provide information about these cruises.

Loch Morar also claims to have a monster but either it is

too quiet or the scattering of people in the area are not publicity conscious. Personally I would advise anyone not to worry over-much about whether Morar has a monster or not. I would counsel rather a readiness to see and admire one of the loveliest of settings in the whole of the Highland area.

There are many other inland lochs each with its own special delight and particular appeal, each making the man who sees it for the first time believe that he and he alone is capable of the deep appreciation for the beauty which he has discovered and which will always hold a secret corner in his heart.

The sea lochs, those incomparable fjords bringing a part of the universal ocean to reach deep into the west coast, have an altogether and an unmistakeably different character from the soft fresh-water inland lochs. True, there are times when the sea lochs can seem soft and times when the bigger inland lochs can be whipped into a fury but, somehow, the smell of the sea, the sight and smell of the russet-brown fringes of seaweed on the shores are a subconscious reminder that there is power and strength in these sea lochs and even a threat for those who would be careless.

The Clyde, with its routh of familiar lochs—Long, Goil, Gare, Holy, Striven, Gilp and Fyne, and of course the Kyles of Bute—is a yachtsman's and a sea fisherman's paradise for the people who live in the cities and towns developed by that busy river. "Doon the watter" was the old phrase for going on annual holiday. It meant among other things taking or even, for a party, chartering one of the steamers which were either devoted to pleasure or could take time off from the daily routine of ferrying passengers across the estuary. The phrase is still used to signify the annual holiday but at least one generation of Clydesiders, if not two, have still to have the fun of going on a ship's cruise round these lovely lochs and

101

to be awakened to the heritage of beauty awaiting for them just round the corner from their own back door. As a consequence of the railway nationalisation, the handful of small shipping fleets competing for the Firth of Clyde traffic were also nationalised. A few things happened as a result. The gay little ships with their individual liveries were all painted alike. There was a long tradition of itinerant musicians aboard the ships; they carried a piano aboard and produced a fiddle and a melodeon. Then, after cheerfully serenading the passengers, they passed round the hat. The new rail authorities put a stop to that begging on board their ships.

So there we were. The colours were reduced to sameness and a natural and quite acceptable form of humble music-making was eliminated. I keep hoping that British Rail will some day try the experiment of putting back the varied colour and will let the music return. I keep hoping too that they will also analyse the market, now untapped, which "doon the watter" could provide if the cruising potential of the Clyde's sea lochs were re-exploited along lines which appealed to the children and grandchildren who know the old phrase but have not yet enjoyed the present reality.

From the Clyde north to Cape Wrath and along the northern shore of Sutherland there is a great profusion of sea lochs each with its own compelling charm and each with its own devotees. There are superb rewards of scenery and peace for the man who leaves the beaten track and finds his own special corner of beauty. But even for the motorist who may only too often get a mere glimpse in passing there is Loch Etive where, as he crosses the old railway bridge at Connel Ferry, he can see the strength of the tidal flow in the Falls of Lora; or Loch Leven at Ballachulish where he can look east to the hills guarding Glencoe or west to a glorious panorama of sea and mountain.

There is now a bridge between South and North Ballachulish but I would counsel the motorist to get out of his car as he used to do while waiting for the ferry, stretch his legs, expand his lungs with clean air, and fill his eyes and mind with the beauty and strength of the scene. He can also, if he is so minded (and he ought to be), scramble up the little knoll at South Ballachulish just across the road from the ferry slipway. There on top of that knoll he will find a historic and unusual memorial to mark the execution on that spot of James Stewart of the Glen for, says the inscription, "a crime of which he was not guilty." It is a reminder, amidst the beauty, of the passions aroused by the Appin Murder when Colin Campbell, the Red Fox, was murdered and James Stewart, protesting his innocence, was tried at Inveraray before a jury of fifteen, of whom eleven were Campbells. To this day, there are people in Appin who say that they know who the murderer was but no one will tell. The gun which fired the shot was known as "The Black Gun of Misfortune" and, if you visit Jimmie McGuffie's popular Edinburgh restaurant, The Doric, he will show you what he believes to be the very gun but he won't tell where it came from or all that he knows about that faraway murder. You can read or re-read Robert Louis Stevenson's *Kidnapped*, with its central theme of the murder, and you still will not know who fired the fatal shot. But you can climb that knoll at South Ballachulish and read on that memorial the poignant echo of crime and injustice.

To the west and north lie the sea lochs all waiting to be explored and found afresh. To the west of Oban there is Loch Aline in the Sound of Mull where there is a commercial operation to take out silica sand for glass-making. At the other end of the Sound, Loch Sunart winds its way into Inverness-shire to provide a magnificent day's sailing. Near

Salen, on the north shore, I once went to see the county roadman who was a weekly contributor to the *Oban Times* and the *Weekly Scotsman*, and who conducted a world-wide correspondence about place-names and clan backgrounds. His cottage stood on a little spit of ground right on the lochside looking south to shapely Ben Resipol on the other shore. The cottage door was beginning to rot at the bottom. There were unclean milk bottles on a window shelf. The place looked unkempt, a rural slum amid the surrounding beauty. He eventually came to the door in his stocking soles showing great holes. He hadn't shaved for days and my heart sank. Then we began to talk and after a sentence or two I forgot the squalor and became conscious only of two bright blue eyes and a keen intelligent mind. It was an experience and I was glad I had stopped to talk to him.

On the way north to Skye are Lochs Nevis and Hourn, the lochs of heaven and hell, each in magnificent wild settings, and each a place where travel by boat is the best form of transport.

Up in Ross-shire, Loch Broom is becoming more popular year by year largely as a result of the sea-angling festivals at Ullapool, which have attracted a faithful following from the Geordies of Northumberland where sea fishing is a religion which grips whole families.

But of all the lochs I have seen whether large or small, whether inland or sea, few have more attraction for me than Tannoch Loch in Milngavie, just north of Glasgow. In the background about four miles away is a splendid backdrop formed by the Campsie Hills. Tannoch is quite small with about thirty houses around it, of which some twenty have their gardens going down to the water. My own house was one of those with a lochside garden. Few settings for a house

104

could have been more idyllic. Small though the loch is it has swans, mallard, coot and water hen. From the kitchen sink, there was always movement of some kind to be seen. During the long summer days there were always boats in the water. It was there that my children learned how to row and handle boats before they went to school. The loch was shallow at the bottom of our garden and I built an island for the children with stepping stones out to it. It was an interesting point that visiting children kept falling or stumbling into the water while the children who grew up alongside the water never did although they used to tear through the gardens and fairly race into the boats. Not once did they put a foot wrong.

That, perhaps, is the greatest boon from living near a loch whether fresh or salt water. Lessons are learned early and the small adventures can lead naturally and smoothly, with confidence, to the greater tests on the bigger waters.

CHAPTER SIX

Once more upon the waters! Yet once more!
And the waves bound beneath me as a steed
That knows his rider.

THIS chapter is largely an account of my own adventures in taking a kayak over the Minch. It was the first solo crossing but much of that kind of adventuring is now commonplace and is taken for granted. My justification for this account is that, although some incidents have been recounted previously in writing and on the air with the B.B.C., the story with its attendant encounters has not been told in coherent detail.

For an account of the preliminary adventures, anyone interested should consult *Quest by Canoe* by Alastair M. Dunnett. My story is a sequel and really begins with the intervening year when I was working in London. Most of my weekends were spent with the Camping Club of Great Britain, Canoeing Section, on their site on the Thames at Chertsey. Some weekends were organised as tours of rivers and canals with delightful, memorable journeys as a result. On one of these tours when we were in a lovely backwater with a peaceful appealing little village and a local which we were about to visit, one of our party—a Londoner and a graduate of London University—looking at the riparian pastoral with some disdain, said to me, "I shouldn't care to live anywhere where my centre wasn't London," and then she added a question, "Would you?" I answered bluntly, "My centre isn't London." I know it was ungracious but it was true and it "gart" me

109

think. Subconsciously I knew I was in the wrong place but having at least to define where my place was not forced me to ask myself if I should be elsewhere. Yet I enjoyed these weekends, particularly those spent at Chertsey, and I got to know some splendid people—the Unwins, Roy McCarthy and many others. Of my own compatriots there were Alastair Knight Craighead, a vigorous C.A., reared in Aberdeen, who was later to become Managing Director of Allied Ironfounders; Ronuill MacInnes, his brother-in-law, who had a successful glass-container manufacturing business, and Donald Macpherson from Barra, then a policeman in the London force and who, with his wife, later ran a hotel in Comrie, Perthshire. It was while there was a discussion about the Hebrides with some of the Londoners that Donald made an observation which again made me think. "Yes," he said, "it can be as warm in Barra in the Outer Hebrides as it is here but it isn't so oppressive; even on the hottest days there is always a breeze from the sea." This conversation took place on a very hot day in Chertsey and we were in and out of the canoes and the river in pleasant languorous and sensual enjoyment of the sun and the warm muddy brown water. It made me think of the tang of the clean western sea and it helped me decide. No man can be really happy living in one place while his heart is in another.

A fortnight after leaving the warm brown Thames I was in my kayak off the coast of Skye and the whole world sang. The sea was clean and clear, the air was keen and invigorating, all around me was a landscape of captivating beauty. I was back to where I belonged along with my heart.

From Kyle of Lochalsh, over to Kyleakin and up past Scalpay to Portree was an easy journey. It helped to get me in tune with the lift and smack of the waves and gave me a chance to practise some of the smoother techniques I had learned in the south. I was young and fit and God was good. I was committed to an adventure in my own country and I was going to complete on my own the crossing which Alastair Dunnett and I had had to postpone the year before.

The adventure came early. The next morning as I was being seen off from Portree by quite a crowd, one of the teachers from the Portree High School whispered in my ear, "It's the general opinion here you'll never see Staffin to-night." On the face of it, the pessimism seemed justified. Although Portree Bay was sheltered, the day was dull and cold. The wind was from the north; the eighteen miles of cliff and rock between me and Staffin offered no shelter or haven for the night if I were to find the going too stiff, and my fourteen-foot canvas kayak looked too fragile for the seas that the Sgianachs knew I would meet outside the bay. When I poked my nose out of the sheltered bay and turned north I realised the point of the comment. A half gale was blowing straight down the Sound of Raasay with nothing from the North Pole to break or ease it except me and my canoe. The sea was short, steep and fast, as unpleasant as it could be and, if I had had any sense, I would have turned back to Portree. But the hardest thing for any young man to face is someone saying smugly, "I told you you couldn't do it." It had to be Staffin.

I had the Sound to myself and to begin with I exulted in the savage splendour after the laxy weekends on the sluggish Thames. The canoe never at any time had way on her and had to be lifted into movement with each stroke of the paddle. It was dip and heave, dip and heave, hour after hour, every thrust coming up from feet braced hard against the bulkhead through straining arms gripping hard on the double-bladed paddle.

The fast moving sea and the quick succession of waves gave the impression of speed, but I had only to look at the cliffs to see how slowly I was covering the miles. Holm Island was a long time in reaching me. I rested in its lee for half an hour while, paddles athwart the canoe to steady it in the lifting swell, I ate my sandwiches as Holm Island heaved and sank beside me.

Eilean nan Gobhar—island of the goats—was the name someone had given me for Holm Island and it was no misnomer. There was the goat with a kid on a narrow ledge not far from where I rested, giving back my stare of interest. I was surprised to see it on what appeared from my fish's eye view to be a most inhospitable mound of rock, and the goat eyed me as though the presence of a human bobbing about in a canoe off the island confirmed her belief in the superior intelligence of the lesser creation.

The thought of leaving the comparative shelter of the island to take up the battle northward made no great appeal, but a survey of the camping possibilities showed no way of getting on to the island from the canoe and no shelter for a tent for the night. Skyewards was no better. Not a scrap of bay or cove offered itself. The choice was still one of on to Staffin or back to Portree.

So on to Staffin again it was in an unbroken toiling at the paddles, striving to make headway against the unending succession of crests gripping at the canoe to carry it southwards.

The effort expended on each stroke and the growing monotony of it after eight hours brought on a weariness that surged up into a near panic when dusk came and it began to look as if it would be dark before I reached Staffin Bay. The prospect of spending another eight hours keeping right side up throughout the night until dawn would light me to a safe landing was unpleasing enough to put fresh vigour into my strokes.

Weariness dropped away when I saw I was rounding a point and entering a bay. It was too dark to see what the shore looked like, but the cottage lights of Staffin shone from the hill. The soft golden gleams in the gathering night would have lured me in to risk any rocky disaster. I piled the canoe in and heard, with a great relief, her bottom grinding in sand.

It took only seconds to heave her on to the wrack out of reach of the tide and to grab my kit and change of clothes. The end of a tiring day on the sea in a canoe is no time for relaxing. Reaction from the physical effort sets in quickly. In dirty weather, every stitch of clothes is soaking with salt water and the chill that strikes when one steps from the canoe is instantaneous.

The imperative need is to change into dry clothes at speed and then at leisure to think of warm food.

The lateness of my arrival put me against camping and I decided to try to put up in one of the cottages overnight.

Just up the shore from me on the machair, a boy was rounding up cattle for the night. I hurried to him to ask if he could direct me to a house that would take me in. When he heard the voice and saw me approaching out of the dusk from the sea, he let out a cry and took to his heels. He must have thought me a queer sort of bogle, maybe even an *each uisge.** I ran after him for a few paces before I realised that that would scare the wee chap out of his wits, so I stopped and called him.

After a bit, I was able to convince him that I was human, although I was not at all sure that he understood much English. He led me to his mother's cottage, where, shivering

* Water horse

113

with the cold as though in a high fever, I explained that I wanted a room for the night.

She, good woman, rose to my need and despatched one of her brood to make enquiries of a neighbour, with the injunction "*agus ruith. Tha e fliuch.*"* An understatement, I thought, but it set her wee lad off at the run, and I was shortly thereafter brought to a cottage and shown into an upstairs bedroom where I could change.

With commendable thoughtfulness and speed a basin of hot water was produced. I stripped, towelled hard, and then laved my warming body with the hot water. I put one foot in the basin and splashed the soothing warmth on my leg. Then I thought it would be a good idea if I got both feet in and stood in the water. The basin, which was small, was one of those china affairs, and I had scarcely put my weight on when it cracked with a sound like the crack of doom and broke in two. The water poured over the floor like a tide.

I could hear it running through the floorboards and trickling down into the room below, but a stranger in a house, stripped to the buff and dripping wet, is in no state to raise an immediate alarm. I threw on a shirt and kilt and hurried downstairs to get a cloth and apologise. Fortunately there was a sense of humour under that roof.

After the strain of the journey, my heart thumped too much that night for me to sleep soundly. Next day was a Sunday, a quiet, sunny day, and I took it easy—in any case, travelling on Sundays in Skye is not regarded with favour.

I sat on a hillside in the calm of the morning sun and soaked myself in the peace and mellow colour of the island. Autumn was burning the bracken and smearing the green of the

* And run. He's wet.

pastures with vivid patches of rich brown. Rocks and cliffs on the shores stood purple against the blue of the Sound, now lapping innocently into Staffin Bay. Beyond where the island stretched a last finger north in Rudha Hunish, I could see the island group of Fladda Chuain. Beyond them again, somewhere into the haze, lay Harris and Lewis over the Minch. Behind me, the hills of Ross and Sutherland held up from their peaks long rolls of fleece-white cumulus clouds.

As I sat on that hill in Skye considering the quiet of the sea I would rather have seen it rough. At that time of the year, the weather often alternates from good to bad on successive days, and that calm Sunday at Staffin with its threat of dirty weather on Monday scared the life out of me—and my heart was still thumping.

I intended crossing the Minch on Monday and liked the idea less and less as the day wore on. The crofter I was staying with was discouragingly pessimistic and urged me strongly not to try it. He, too, mistrusted the calm of the day. But that did not prevent him from seeing me off on Monday morning with advice on tides and routes.

His specific advice was succinct, "Kilmaluag is four miles up the coast. You should stay there." It was kindly meant and I would have liked to pay my respects to the resting place of Flora MacDonald, but an hour later I was well past Kilmaluag and sensing with anticipation the opening into the wide Minch. Round Rudha Hunish and there were the little isles of Fladda Chuain ahead and on the horizon the low silhouettes of the Outer Isles twenty miles away. It was in my mind that it might be interesting to land on the Fladda Chuain but there was a strong north tide and it was soon clear that I was going to be carried two miles or so to the north of them and that it would be ill-advised to waste effort

115

on counteracting the tidal flow. In any case, I was by then getting my first experience of overfalls miles off shore and I didn't like it. Overfalls are caused by strong tides passing over major variations of height in the sea bed. The effect is to produce a turbulent area of white water in the middle of nowhere. The turbulence seems to have no positive direction of flow. The waves set up appear to be moving in all directions and, in a small craft, one gets an impression of determined supernatural malevolence; until one moves out of the overfalls area and the sea subsides.

Crossing the Minch was tedious, an endurance test rather than an exciting journey. As the hills of Skye grew smaller and the hills of Harris grew larger I hopefully estimated at one point that I must be half-way. Then a Baltic timber ship came down from the north and as she passed between me and Harris my heart sank a little. All I could see was her super-structure and I knew I had still a long way to go. Sitting low down in a canoe, the visible horizon is between two and four miles but even so—only to see the superstructure meant that there were more sea miles to travel than the eye imagined.

It was some weary hours later before the lighthouse of Scalpay, Harris, became distinguishable—bobbing around my bow as the waves lifted me. That was heartening, at least, for it indicated that my very rough and ready dead reckoning had me dead on course. Still later I saw the Sgeir-i-noe lightship tumbling and rolling and then I began to hear the monotonous sound of its disconsolate bell constantly tolling. It was a gloomy sound and I heard it for a long time before I finally began to round the island of Scalpay. As I neared the island, two lobster fishermen were coming out. They veered over to me and gave me a hail. "We'll tow you in for ten sheelings," they offered. It seemed an inadequate welcome.

116

It was a chastened pioneer who declined the bargain and pushed on alone to a landfall.

Scalpay is a small island, lying off Tarbert, where they earn their living from the sea and it was one of the few islands where the population was increasing. The welcome I got from the lobster fishermen was not typical and the kindly islanders were quick to show that they had all the traditional instincts for hospitality. I slept two nights in my tent perched on a knoll looking over the Sound of Harris; then Norman Mac-Leod, the local merchant, put a stop to camping by bringing me in at night to sleep under his bien roof. Before that, he had already put a stop to my cooking for myself. Norman was proud of having water on tap in his house—you would have to see how low-lying, rocky and waterless Scalpay is to appreciate that apparent miracle. It puzzled me and he was happy as a schoolboy to be able to explain that the water was rainwater collected from the roof (as in Bermuda) into a storage tank and fed by gravity to the taps.

"But," I asked him, for his house stood on the water's edge and I saw a snag, "don't you get spray on the roof?" "We do, often," he replied, "sometimes you can taste the salt." It was clear that he regarded a trifling matter like an occasional seasoning of sea salt as bringing no blemish on his island version of mod. con.

Scalpay is no more than three miles wide at the most but it was a day's job to cross it. At each door, I was stopped to pass the time of day and then invited in for a cup of tea. Only a churl could have refused the courtly invitations and I progressed from fireside to fireside on a sea of tea. Strong black tea it was, poured from teapots which sat hottering on the hob throughout the day. In each house I had to eat a home-baked scone or oatcake with crowdie. For the benefit

117

of the uninitiated, crowdie is a simple form of cheese. Thick sour milk is heated slowly until the whey separates and can be strained off. The solid is seasoned with salt and pepper and eaten as a cream cheese.

It was on Scalpay that I met an old crofter fisherman long beyond the age for deep-sea fishing who asked me, "Were you ever in Peterhead?" I told him that I had indeed been in Peterhead and he gave me this delicious comment in the soft and precisely enunciated English of the Gaelic speaker. "Not many of the people of Scalpay have been there, but I have. They speak a funny language. You could take any of the people of Scalpay to Peterhead and they would not understand one word of what was being said. But I would. I can speak their language. It's like broken English."

I have treasured that story since the day I heard it from the old man as we stood beside his cottage in a setting of outstanding beauty. Behind us lay the hills of Harris already showing brown under the September sun. In front of us to the south west across the silent, silver sea of the Hebrides, the Cuillins of Skye reached upwards towards their crowns of cloud. The old man's travelling with the herring fleet among the strange people on the east coast was done, and he had come home to his own people to rest in the lovely setting of his own island and there await his last call from the Fisher of Men.

When I meet anyone from other parts of the country who affects amusement at the speech of the Highlander, I tell the old man's story to sting them with its reproof. "Broken English" is a fair taunt to the Lowlander who mocks the Gael and I, who was reared in the broad tongue which sounded so queer to the Hebridean ear, feel free to use the taunt.

Staunch Wee Free Scalpay has one point in common with

118

the devout Catholics of Barra at the foot of the Outer Isles. On Sunday, the peace of these two islands becomes intensified as all servile work stops and all prepare to go to church to worship the same God in their different ways. It is fashionable nowadays to poke fun at devotion and to complain on behalf of the tourist over interruptions to traffic and commercial services, but it is this change of pace, this adjustment of attitudes which can give the Highlands and Islands their attraction. In a frenetic world, we can all benefit from the example of quiet people who, from time to time, live the Biblical injunction—be still and know that I am God.

When I finally managed to tear myself away from Scalpay, it was to head north up that magnificent fjord of Loch Seaforth which runs 14 to 15 miles from its mouth in Harris to its head in Lewis. It is over three miles wide at its mouth and narrows to a quarter of a mile before it opens into a hammer head four miles long. At the narrows there is a rocky shoal where the tidal current can run as fast as eight miles an hour and make a roar which in calm weather can be heard for miles. I had, of course, studied the charts and gazetteers and was well aware of this tide rip but the weather, which was worsening, finally broke down in a furious burst of rain and hail as I approached the narrows. I had been counting on good visibility to help me see the main current flows and to avoid rocks, but the force of the rain stotting off the loch raised such a misty cloud of splashes that it was impossible to see where the rain ended and the loch began. I had to leave it to my canoe and the flood water to carry me via the safer channels. I swept through into the hammer head of the loch and the storm ceased. I could not have been wetter if I had couped the kayak.

On the north shore of the loch there was a solitary house. I put the bow of the canoe on to it and fairly drove ashore.

It was another occasion, I felt, when the tent was not big enough or warm enough for the stripping, drying and changing I had to face. The two strapping brothers who lived by themselves showed me with some concern into their spare room. A change into warm clothes made all the difference. Next day I got the bus and, with the canoe on top, made a portage in comfort to Loch Erisort from where the next stage of the journey to Stornoway was uneventful.

It was a farmer who met me at the pier to congratulate me on the Minch crossing, and while I was in Stornoway had me out to his farm on a number of occasions to meet his family of lively daughters. Stornoway is lively all round and no one there would have thought anything of the under-age Prince Charles having a quick cherry brandy. Indeed, nothing would have been heard about that celebrated schoolboy tipple if an over-eager young journalist hadn't blabbed. One must remember that the puritanical restrictions in the Highlands do not extend to whisky, the *uisge beatha* or water of life, and its associated alcoholic beverages.

I had been instructed by her family in Edinburgh to call on District Nurse Meg McIvor and in the course of several conversations with her was asked if I could help her to put down on paper some of the verses she enjoyed composing. The Gaelic I had so far learned was fairly elementary but I said I would try if she would give me a word at a time so that I could take it down phonetically and then try to get the correct spelling. It was a fascinating exercise. She had given me only the first few words when I realised that her sense of liaison in speech was so strong that each "word" she was giving me was the end of one word and the beginning of the next. She had no picture in her mind of the shapes of words in her native tongue.

120

On reflection then and since, I felt it damnable that an intelligent young woman could grow up in a Gaelic-speaking area and be denied, for any reason, the birthright to be literate in her native tongue. But neglect of the native Highland tongue still continues. Gaelic speakers need to fight harder than they do for proper recognition of the language. There is an adventure in that fight ready to hand for a group of young people who could well copy the determination which young people in Wales are showing in fighting to preserve a cognate language. Not all of the things done by the young Welsh can be condoned but, stage by stage, Welsh is being accorded parity with English in Welsh-speaking Wales. We are passionate about much in Scotland but we are lacking in the fire which might yet save a language that goes deep into our heritage.

For four years, when I was Managing Director of the *Chester Chronicle* and its associated papers, I lived in Chester and had several Welsh-speaking colleagues on my staff. One of the editions circulates extensively in North Wales and the use of Welsh in its columns is natural. I made it my business to learn a little of the language and then was given an additional spur. Each year the President of the Caledonian Association is a guest speaker at the St David's Day Dinner. I attended the St David's Day dinner while I was in Chester. I was impressed by the vigorously bi-lingual character of the function and dismayed by the monoglot performance of the Scots who spoke. When my turn came during the year when I was president of the Caledonian Association I made it my goal to deliver my St David's Day contribution in Welsh with Gaelic words thrown in for good measure. It was not of a high linguistic standard but it was a gesture which required to be made and which was appreciated by the Welsh who, by fiery dedication, have saved their language by insisting on its use. Would to God that we had even a touch of that flame.

We have, however, kept our songs and our piping. Our musical tradition is safe. When I was in Stornoway I renewed acquaintance with Duncan Morrison, a native of Stornoway and a pianist of rare distinction. For some reason, Duncan was nicknamed The Major and again in the south of England I identified a Hebridean by his nickname. It was during the war and in the course of a Signals Corps exercise I found myself in the evening in a tiny village pub. Don't ask me where it was. We got there in the blackout and I have only a general impression that it was in Dorset or Somerset. Anyway, there was a young woman in a party and I was introduced to her. She was very ill-at-ease but after a sentence or two I traced her accent to Stornoway. She refused to believe that the fellow in the badly-fitting battledress could possibly know Stornoway. I mentioned some names including Duncan Morrison's. She still refused to believe me until I said "The Major." At that, a look of horror came on her face and shortly afterwards she left. I realised that her unease came from finding herself in a den of iniquity like an English pub. She was prepared to put up with it as long as she felt she was anonymous but, when I used a nickname which suggested that I might even be a means of her parents knowing about the pub visit, it was too much for her.

Some nicknames defy logic. There were two brothers MacDonald who answered one to "MacKay" and the other to "MacKenzie." The ridiculous point is that where they lived the name MacDonald was uncommon but every second man was a MacKenzie and the others were MacKays.

One west Highland township had a "Holy Willie" so called, I was told, because he was "the only one we know of in the island." It also had a "Calum Innocent" and an "Alasdair

122

Naomh" (Gaelic for pure). One fellow-citizen, well known to all three was credited with a comment worthy of Diogenes. "There are," said he "three men in this town I have never met, Holy Willie, Calum Innocent and Alasdair Naomh."

Jimmie MacKenzie, coal merchant in Stornoway, was a remarkable, ebullient character. Very early on in our acquaintance he startled me by saying, "I'll lend you a gun, if you like." He had just shown me his armoury. There was a double-bore shotgun which had belonged to his father before him. He handled it with the reverence due to a fine piece in Damascus steel. There was worship in his voice as he pulled the plugs of wadding from the barrel and invited me to look through the spotless bore. His rifles ·22 and ·40 had the same sleek oily appearance of treasured possessions carefully tended. Our talk passed from guns to shooting, from stags to salmon, for he regarded "lifting" as one of the finer forms of art in sport. Shooting salmon on the leap he enjoyed as a nice combination of marksmanship and clever boat sense, but stalking what he called the "big stuff," by night and early morning, appealed to his idea of the rights and duties of a man. "It's no sin to lift a deer," he defined, not in extenuation, but as a statement of the correct and only attitude.

Jimmie had his own unique comment on the Lord Leverhulme episode. Lord Leverhulme conceived the idea that he could improve the fishing and farming in Lewis and Harris by bringing to the task a business organisation and, in so doing, he would also improve the standard of living in the island. His idea was right but his approach was wrong. After one meeting with some of the people at which he explained what he was going to do for them in, amongst other things, better housing, he received a celebrated and dignified rebuke from one old crofter who spoke for the meeting. "Lord

123

Leverhulme," said the crofter. "We give you credit for your good intentions. But you referred to our houses as hovels. I would remind you that to us they are our homes." The whole of that period makes a fascinating study. The Hebrides where security of land tenure had been achieved again after the brutal interregnum of the Highland Clearances was the only part of Great Britain where the poor man could, in fact, subsist by his own efforts and therefore was not under compulsion to accept an outsider's reorganisation of his way of life. The reaction to Lord Leverhulme's proposals was based on the security of personal independence and was a quiet but firm rejection. Jimmie's comment and protest were more ebullient. "Lord Leverhulme bought the island and the cattle and the sheep and he thought he could buy me," he told me, "and one Saturday he had a party in Stornoway Castle and all the people of Stornoway were there, but I I wasn't. I was out in the bay shooting his salmon."

Jimmie MacKenzie's standard of the fitness of things was based entirely on "lifting." He looked at my canoe, mentally measuring the carcase of a hind into the cockpit. "No," and he dismissed the canoe from the category of practical boats, "It's no use. It's too small for anything."

Later, in a generous outburst, he offered to lend me a gun. To him that was the height of hospitality and he followed it with the offer of a revolver for he could not conceive any happiness in my travelling without the weapons of real enjoyment. I thought, at first, that his was the extreme expression of the spirit of the Highlands, defying the comparatively recent game laws by the exercise of an age-old right; but I met others, plenty of them, who made me similar offers and I gathered that it is hardly the thing to travel the islands, during the stalking season, without a gun.

The deer-stalking season happens to coincide with a slack season on the crofts, a happy coincidence which ensures the greatest possible enjoyment to the greatest possible number. It is not only in the Big House that they are busy cleaning and oiling the guns. They do a little of that on the crofts too.

In Lewis most of the crofters are staunch Wee Frees. Their grace before meat is a long supplication during which the food on the table congeals to an unappetising lukewarmness. The grace after meat is scarcely shorter but not much time elapses after the final amen, before the stranger is questioned about his gun. Even in the Wee Free manse it will be an unusual tea if, in the course of it, the minister fails to ask, "Have you a gun with you?"

It is no exaggeration to say that, in many of the islands, there are people who are surfeited with salmon and venison. "I grow sick at the sight of salmon," one woman said to me, but her husband, with a glitter in his eyes, said, "It's in the blood. If I had a bead on a stag I'd let the beggar have it although all the keepers in creation were beside him."

When I was leaving Jimmie MacKenzie, I suggested that next year I would be back with a bigger boat and a gun which I would submit to him for his approval. He brushed that aside as unnecessary. "You bring the boat," he promised, "and I'll see you all right for guns."

Two incidents reminded me of the hazards of the sea and that it was time to be on the way back from Stornoway. A Baltic timber ship whose deck cargo had shifted in bad weather was towed into the bay. Only the fact that her cargo was timber kept her from capsizing. A RAF flying boat made a bad landing in North Bay and very nearly sank.

As I made my preparations for heading back south, Captain Stewart, an old salt, drew me aside and pointed up to the sky. "Look," said he, "mackerel backs and mares' tails make lofty ships carry low sails. There's a lot of wind there. Don't go to-day."

But I was ready to go and I intended to travel only a few miles and then duck into Loch Erisort. It was rough— rougher than the stretch from Portree to Staffin. The wind was from the south and once more in my teeth. The seas were short, steep and powerful but, by then, my muscles and hands had hardened and, knowing that it was a short journey, I enjoyed it until I got to Ranish.

I thought that Ranish was different when I put ashore from the canoe. The folk, who stopped working at their potatoes to watch, gave me no answering wave. No one hurried down, eager to help the stranger. The atmosphere of reticence seemed almost to resent my presence. However, the weather was wild outside and Ranish, at the head of the loch and more sheltered than the stormy Minch, seemed the most suitable place to spend the night in the rising gale. Later, when I had changed into dry clothes, I took my bundle of soaking canoeing garments to the nearest house to ask if they would dry them over the fire for me anent the morn's canoeing. The reply took me aback. "Put them out on the grass in the wind!"

As I went down the road again, buttoning my oilskin tightly around me to keep out the driving rain, I thought that over. The traditional warm Highland hospitality was scarcely hot in Ranish. True enough, during the afternoon, I was invited into one house for a cup of tea and made very welcome but, by nightfall, the bars were up against me in the whole village.

The rain came lashing across the hillside and, behind it, the wind driving hard. One moment my wee tent was billowing out like a balloon, the next it was blown flat until the sides met.

The groundsheet and most of my kit were already wet. It was THE night, I decided, for a roof over my head. But the coolness of earlier on developed into a definite frigidity. Doors were opened slightly while the folk behind them peered out at me where I stood in the rain-slashed darkness, such light as escaped through the mere crack of open doorway shining wet from my oilskin. At each house my reception was much the same. "I'm sorry," the person sheltering behind the door would say, "No, I'm sorry." And then they would close the door again—on the wind, the rain, and me.

While I waited outside one house the wind, whirling through a gap in the hills and whistling round the house, found the water barrel. Waves leaped and spouted even there. I was able to smile at that storm in a barrel and feel sorry for myself at the same time. But the woman of the house had no humour. Her face was grim and her "no" was hard and final. I gave it up then.

Whatever it was that ailed them, they certainly did not like my looks in Ranish and I walked two wet and windy miles to the next village to find a hospitable roof. The woman who took me in did so with the chastening remark, "Come in. I wouldn't keep the tinkers out on a night like this."

I was told in a neighbouring village that the Ranish folk are always suspicious of strangers but I was never able to find out what there was about me that stormy night to close the doors on me. By contrast, a day or two later I put up at a house where the good man, having heard of my experience of Ranish, was excessively anxious to be hospitable. "That's right, boy," he said, as I sat in to the table, "Take your tea now, make yourself at home. You don't need to be afraid of anyone here." He punctuated each phrase by clapping me on the back in a nice friendly way. He was, however, about

127

eighteen stones in weight and his slaps were hearty swings from the shoulder that almost felled me. Then the son of the house appeared. "That's right, boy. Take your tea," he began, fetching me skelps almost as heavy as his father's. It was a hearty household and it filled up with neighbours in the evening. It was an enjoyable evening of good humour and the kind of informed conversation which is the hallmark of the islanders, many of whom are world travellers returned home.

It was a long plod next day down Loch Seaforth enlivened by a period of extreme thoughtfulness when, in the middle of the loch, I realised that I was taking in water. When I got ashore to have a look I saw that, when I had been giving the crofters joy rides the previous evening, the canvas had been cut by their method of launching. This was to sit in while the others pushed, heaved and hauled the canoe into a sufficient depth of water. Fortunately the six-inch cut was along the length of one of the frame timbers and water pressure on canvas and timber prevented the leak developing. I was relieved when I had the patch secure for the weather was worsening and the wind was rising. Before I got down the length of Loch Seaforth I had one further bout of meditation. Away down the loch I saw a huge black shape and a huge black fin coming up very fast almost motionless as though it were mechanically propelled. I saw it veer towards me and I promptly stopped paddling and tried to look like a piece of flotsam. It worked and again I was relieved. I assumed it to be a sailfish, an inquisitive and sometimes aggressive fish which had a name for damaging small craft and even drifters.

By the time I reached the mouth of Loch Seaforth, the weather was bad. The narrows of Scalpay were as wild as anything I had seen, white from shore to shore, a malevolent,

128

turbulent maelstrom. I had no choice. I had to try it but I was not altogether confident that this time I was not trying too much and that I would be able to make it to Scalpay.

The next day on the island an old man said to me, "I was watching you yesterday in Caolas Scalpay. You know, not one of the men of Scalpay would have taken a boat out in that sea." It was a tribute from one boatman to another and I treasured it.

The following day when I carried my canoe on to Mac-Brayne's ship at Tarbert for the journey back to Glasgow, one of the ship's engineers looked down scornfully over the lovely, fragile little kayak as it lay on the deck, and declared, "There are far more scientific ways of travelling than that."

Ah, well.

CHAPTER SEVEN

Oh, aye, they'll be makin' fun o's again.

ANY observation of the Scot would lack a major dimension if it did not include a closer look at what makes him laugh and at how he says the things which seem to him to have wit and humour. Most of his humour is direct although some may be oblique. It may be grim or earthy or irreverent but it is rarely sleazy. I have chosen the stories which follow because they seem to me to be representative. They may not make you laugh outright, for much depends on the way they are spoken, but they ought to give you a quiet smile to yourself and, that, I would regard as a demonstration of the authenticity of the idiom.

The Scot accepts with Ecclesiastes the Preacher that there is a time to be born and a time to die, a time to weep and a time to laugh but he tends to disguise some of his deepest emotions in macabre jokes. For the Scot, there is always a time for a sardonic comment on the continuing human comedy, especially in its more solemn implications. Death, for him, does not always have a sting. And some of his best stories are about death:

Three old men were sitting on a hillside on a beautiful summer's evening, peacefully smoking their pipes while they gazed down on the village spread before them in the calm of the evening light. Just below them was the kirkyard with its venerable graves and, as they looked at it, they fell naturally to contemplating man's latter end. Eventually, the eldest took his pipe out of his mouth and said, "Aye. When my time comes, ye can put me doon alangside Jock Scott. We had mony a guid nicht at the salmon thegither."

There was a long silence while they pondered that pleasant prospect and then the one in the middle took his pipe out and said, "Weel, when it's my turn, ye can lay me wi' Sandy MacDonald. Mony's the guid dram we had thegither."

After a shorter silence, the youngest of the trio took his pipe out and said, "I'd like to be doon there beside Jeannie Broon."

The other two turned on him and said irritably, "But Jeannie Broon's no' deid yet."

"No," was his reply, "and neether am I."

When the Connel Ferry was running, a tourist, impressed by the tidal swirl, asked the ferryman if he ever lost many passengers.

"No," said Donald, "we mostly find them again doon aboot Dunstaffnage."

The two men in the Glasgow pub had been shattered by the sudden death of a friend and workmate. As they drank to his memory and as consolation improved with each drink, one of them suggested calling on the widow. By then, they had had a drink too many and they went up to the house. The widow was a little surprised by the solicitude but asked them inside where they both became tongue tied. To ease the strain, the widow asked, "Would you like to see him?"

It was the last thing they wanted but, as they didn't know how to refuse, they found themselves ben the house looking at their old friend lying on the bed in his coffin. Searching for something to say, one of them burst out with, "My, isn't he awful sunburnt!"

134

"Aye," agreed the widow. "That last wee holiday he had at Rothesay did him a power o' good."

Maggie was on her death bed and she had a last request for John. She wanted him to go to the graveyard in the same car as her mother. She knew that John had never got on with his mother-in-law but it was, she reminded him, the last thing she would ever be able to ask him to do for her.

"A' richt, Maggie," John said eventually and unwillingly. "I'll dae it for your sake, Maggie, but it'll spoil ma day."

The Aberdeen trawler skipper had difficulty in making up his crew and he took on a deckhand who had no experience and who had never been to sea before. The new hand was useless and the crew complained that he was more of a hindrance than a help in rough weather. Eventually, their complaints became so bitter that the skipper said, "Look. Ye ken yersels hoo difficult it is tae get a crew. I ken he hisna been tae sea afore but the laddie'll learn. An I'll tell ye this. He has the grandest references for character. There has never been a mair honest man aboard this boat."

Next day, the new deckhand went to get a bucket of water for the potatoes but, instead of going to the leeside, he went to windward. A huge wave swept him and bucket off the deck. One of the other hands who saw the incident hailed the skipper:

"Hey, skipper. Dae ye mind yon mannie wi' a' the grand references for honesty? Weel, he's awa wi' yer bucket."

*   *   *

The opportunities for jibes at birth and procreation are seized with an earthy vigour. When someone in the south

135

invites me to join him in sniggering at perversion, I tell him that I prefer my country's more robust attitude and, depending on the circumstances, I give him one of the following as an example and a corrective. That may sound pompous and priggish but the stories themselves preserve the balance:

Two men were knocking the stuffing out of each other in the gutter while a wee lad stood on the pavement greetin awfu' sair. A woman passing by asked the boy why he was crying.

"Ma faither's fechtin," he replied.

"Oh dear," said the woman, looking at the two fighting men, "and which is your father?"

"That's what they're fechtin aboot," said the wee lad.

The following conversation is alleged to have been overheard at a Glasgow bus stop:

"Has it came yet?"

"Uh hu"

"Whit is it?"

"A wee girl"

"Whit are they gonna cry it?"

"Hazel"

"Ma Goad, there's a saint for every day o' the year and they have tae go and cry it after a bliddy nut."

The Ayrshire farmer had a family of strapping sons who were itching to make dramatic and, in his eyes, drastic changes on the farm, so he read them a lesson.

"You young fellas," he said, "you're a' the same. Aye wantin tae gae ramstam at a' thing. Ye mind me o' the young bull and the auld bull. The coos had just been lat oot frae the mulkin and the young bull said tae the auld bull, 'Lat's dash up and bull twa o' thae coos' and the auld bull said tae

136

the young bull, 'We'll dae nae sic thing. We'll juist dauner up and bull them a'.''

*   *   *

As everyone in every country who has served in the armed forces knows, the only way to cope with the futility and destruction of war is to preserve the ability to laugh at any uniformed activity at any time. Every army has its own special humour but the examples here are, I think, specific to the Scot:

During the first world war, British insularity was expressed in the joke of the Tommy writing home, "Dear Mum: the French kids are very clever. Long before they go to school, you can hear them playing in the streets and they can all speak French."

The second world war variant of the theme was Scottish. A Glasgow Highlander home on leave was giving his pals a lesson in language:

"See this French, mac? Dead easy. Dead easy. If ye want a couple o' eggs, ye just gae up tae a fermer and say, 'Gie me twa oofs.' Noo, he'll gie ye three and ye gie him wan back."

At the time of the Dunkirk retreat, when the Highland Light Infantry were wearily marching through a battered French village, one of the villagers surveyed them from his doorway which was all that was left of his house. The rest, walls, roof, everything, had been flattened. Only the door and the doorway remained. One of the men raised his weary head, took in the scene, grinned at the recollection of a childhood admonition and said to the villager, "That'll learn ye tae slam the door."

F   137

When the Romans invaded Britain, they did not succeed in conquering Scotland and the local general was very nervous about his reputation being at stake. In one skirmish in Glasgow, he was appalled to see two Glasgow keelies, armed only with cut-throat razors, carving up his legionaries.

"They'll never believe this in Rome," he groaned, "unless I can show them what these keelies are like."

So he gave orders that the two keelies were to be taken alive. After much slaughter, they were, and he triumphantly conveyed them to Rome. A great day in the arena was arranged and savage beasts from all over the empire were brought to face the keelies. On the night before the fight, the two keelies were given a feast and their choice of the damsels. Next morning, they compared notes.

"Hoo did you get on, Jock?" asked Sandy.

"Great," said Jock, "I had a great big smashin' blonde. Oh, she was a right smasher. Efter we had oor chuck, we sat doon wi' muckle goblets o' wine an then we . . ." Jock stopped and took out his razor.

"Go on, Jock. Tell's what happened next."

"I'll tell ye efter," replied Jock. "Here come thae bliddy lions."

When the Highland Division were in for one of their few settled spells, the padre suggested that it would be a good idea to convert a vacant hall into a temporary church. This was done with enthusiasm by the Division whose symbol, HD, was also reckoned to stand for Highway Decorators because of the way they emblazoned their areas. When the padre inspected the church, he found that the decorating enthusiasm had led them to paint the divisional slogan, "Scotland for Ever" over the pulpit. Not wishing to damp enthusiasm or

138

hurt feelings, he admired it but suggested that there might be something more suitable for a church. When he looked in the next morning, the slogan read, "Scotland for Ever and Ever. Amen."

*   *   *

One of our natural aptitudes is the ability to take elements in our history and twist them a little so that the resulting picture, though perhaps less accurate, is much more to our liking. We add our own kind of arrogance by implying that other people, especially the Sasunnach, are stupid if the use of Broad Scots or Gaelic confuses them. The first of these four stories is a classical demonstration of our conceit in our way of speaking and of our overwhelming conceit in ourselves:

When King James the Sixth of Scotland went down to London to become King of Great Britain, he was very much distressed to see the poor people of London going about barefoot. It was all so different from his own country where even the poorest had good woollen hose and stout brogans to their legs and feet. So he called for a trusty English messenger and gave him precise instructions.

"Awa wi' ye up tae ma auld freen, the Loard Proavost o' Edinburry. Tell him I'm gey sair pitten aboot tae see a' thae puir fowk here gaun aboot in their bareys. Tell him that I want him juist as sune as ever he can tae send me doon sax hunder pairs o' brogues. Noo, awa wi ye, man. An hurry."

So off the trusty messenger set, a trifle confused perhaps, but willing. As he skelped north, he couldn't help noticing that the country improved and that the people were better clad. In due course, he clattered into Edinburgh, saw the Lord

139

Provost and delivered the King's command. The King, he said, wanted six hundred pairs of rogues sent down to London and he wanted them in a hurry.

Now that was a poser for the Provost for he knew that the King knew that there weren't six hundred pairs of rogues in Edinburgh, no, nor even in Glasgow, nor, for that matter, in the whole of Braid Scotland. However, he set to work. He emptied the Tolbooth prison. He called for a redding out of the gaols in Glasgow, in Stirling, in Perth, Dundee, Aberdeen and Dumbarton. He scoured the whole country and after great effort he finally gathered together the six hundred pairs of rogues and a fine spectacle of ragtag and bobtail they were as they set out to march to London under the trusty messenger.

At the end of a fortnight's marching, they arrived at the borders of Durham and Yorkshire and had a rest for the week-end. Ragtag though they were, some of them had the right ideas. They cut tree trunks and vied with each other at tossing the cabar. They chose suitable stones and competed at putting the stone. They tuned up the pipes and began to dance. The trusty messenger, who had learned a little of the language by then, was interested to see for the first time a sword dance being performed. One of the competitors was a bit of a cissy and prepared to dance with his shoes on to make sure that he wouldn't cut his toes on the swords and there was a chorus of shouts from the spectators, "Tak aff yer brogues, laddie." The trusty messenger joined in the chorus. "That's right. Take off these bleeding shoes," he shouted and, as he said the words, a penny dropped.

He called his lieutenants together and said, "I say, you chaps, I have dropped a proper clanger. The King wants brogues, not rogues. I'm off back to see the Lord Provost to get the brogues before the King hears about this muck up."

"What are we to do with this lot, then?" asked the lieutenants.

"You do what you like with them. I'm off to Edinburgh," said the trusty messenger.

So the lieutenants turned the six hundred pairs of rogues loose there and then and that is why the people in the north east of England think that they have something in common with the Scots.

In the early eighteenth century, many good men found themselves cooling their heels in the Palais St Germain near Paris with the rest of the Jacobites, unable to return to their native glens. So, from time to time, they drank a toast in an inferior spirit to the country and the people they had left, saluting each other in the old tongue with *Slàinte mhòr a h'uile latha a chi 's nach fhaic*, which can be roughly translated as, "Here's a good health every day that I see you and every day that I don't."

Well, it was a bit of a mouthful and they understandably shortened it occasionally as we do today to *a h'uile la* and that is why the French can now be heard saying, "Oo la la."

A little later, the Highland clearances caused another lot of good men to try their fortunes in Canada. One of them, who had taken an Indian woman as squaw (for as everyone knows the Scot has no racial or colour prejudice), returned wearily to his wigwam or tepee after a fruitless day trudging round his empty traps. As he sat down to take his rawhide brogans off his hot sore feet, his squaw heard him say, *Oh, mo chasan*. So she called his brogues mocassins.

During the last war, many of the Polish soldiers were

141

stationed in the Glasgow area and, eventually, most of them grew to understand the local patois. Occasionally, however, they found themselves baffled.

The bossy wee Glasgow clippie came down the stairs of her tramcar to find the platform crowded with standing passengers. She issued her brisk orders.

"Come oan, youse. Get aff."

The Glaswegians understandingly skailed off the tram. Two Polish officers on the platform looked at her in puzzlement.

"Youse tae," she ordered.

So they stayed where they were and got into terrible trouble.

*   *   *

We have, of course, a routh of whigmaleeries which could be put under various headings, and there are some which defy categorisation, but those which follow have a common element and flavour which seem to me to mark them as sufficiently peculiar to us as to allow us to claim them. They have in full measure the native hallmarks of bluntness in approach and authenticity in idiom:

The London gentleman travelling round Aberdeenshire and the north of Scotland was waiting for the train back south. When the train stopped at his station, he chose an empty first-class compartment, put his bowler and rolled umbrella on the rack, his briefcase on the seat and nipped out to get a copy of the Top People's Paper. When he got back to his compartment, his briefcase was on the rack and all the seats were occupied by six muckle big farmers.

When he had recovered from his first shock of outrage, he addressed them. He had, he said, travelled on railways all over the world and, even in the most primitive uncivilised countries, it was accepted that, when a gentleman put an item of his possessions on the seat, he had reserved that seat.

There was a silence while they contemplated him and his wrath, and then the biggest farmer of the six spoke;

"Imhpm. I've nae doot ye're richt, my mannie. But, in Buchan, it's the doups that coont."

It was at Rothesay that Jock met an old farmer friend, Sandy, who, despite his native canniness, had at last been brought to the altar. After congratulating Sandy, Jock asked how the bride was enjoying the honeymoon.

"Oh," said Sandy, "I didna bring her. She's been in Rothesay afore."

The farmer opened his mail and found that he had a win on the pools.

"Maggie," he said to his wife, "Here's a cheque for a thousand pounds. Is there anything ye wad like?"

"Yes, John, there is," replied Maggie. "I'm tired o' havin tae gae doon the gairden in a' weathers. An, forby, whan we hae veesitors it's no very nice. Can we have it in the hoose?"

"If that's whit ye want, Maggie, I'll dae it," said John.

So it was put in the house. Well, a few months later when John opened his letters he said to his wife:

"Ye'll no believe this, Maggie, but we've won anither thousand pounds on the pools. Is there anything else that ye'd like?"

"There is, John," replied Maggie. "It's a' the rage and a' the neebours have them. I'd like a barbecue."

At the next agricultural show John's farmer friends, having heard of the ongoings, pulled John's leg about the changes he was making for Maggie and John said, "It's an awfu' cairry on this. At wan time we used tae eat in the hoose and gae doon the gairden but noo it's the ither way aboot."

The superior tourist was trying to patronise Donald and was nettled by the way that Donald turned every comment. Finally he saw a straggle of gipsies and tinkers coming round the bend of the road and he said, "And are these some of the local inhabitants, Donald?"

Donald looked round slowly and answered slowly, "No, no. They're just towrists like yourself."

The farm servant had been offered a job by a Lanarkshire farmer but felt that, in honesty, he should explain a point before the farmer committed himself.

"There's juist the ae thing," he said to the farmer, "I've a by-ordnar appetite."

The farmer was offended and stated that he had a reputation for feeding all his people well.

"Aye, but tae lat ye understaun," said the farm servant, "it's like this. For ma breakfast, I tak fower plates o' guid thick porridge wi' twa pints o' creamy milk. Then I'll hae twa or three helpins o' bacon an eggs, plenty o' toast wi' butter and marmalade and plenty o' tea tae wash it doon. For ma denner, I hae sax muckle bowls o' thick broth, fower plates o' tatties an mince, three helpins o' dumplin, a whang o' cheese, a packet o' biscuits an plenty o' coffee tae wash it doon. For ma tea, it's twa punnds o' rashers and a dizzen eggs, lashins o' breid an butter an jam, an plenty o' tea tae wash it doon. Come supper time, I'm no a' that hungry, and a loaf, twa punnds o' butter an three punnds o' cheese 'll dae me."

144

When he finished his litany, he looked expectantly at the farmer and asked, "Weel, dae I get the job?"

"By heavens, no," replied the farmer, "but I'll tell ye what. I'll mak a bargain wi' ye. I'll gie ye £10 a ton for your dung."

They say that the difference between water and whisky is that one of them you must not make in public and the other you must not make in private.

The Marchioness had been walking the estate hills and had had a chat and a cup of tea in his cottage with a lonely shepherd. As she left him, she said, "Now, Thomson. If you are ever in town, you must come and have tea with us. Now, remember, if I ever hear that you have been in London and haven't come to see us, I'll be very annoyed with you."

Well, one day Thomson went down to the Hyde Park sheep dog trials and afterwards set out to pay his respects as ordered. He found the house, knocked on the door, and to the servant who opened it, he said, "Is he in?"

"I beg your pardon," said the servant stiffly. "Do you mean the Marquis?"

"Aye," replied Thomson, "Is he in?"

"I'm sorry," said the servant. "The Marquis is out of town."

"Weel, then," said Thomson. "Is she in?"

"I'm sorry," said the servant. "The Marchioness is engaged, entertaining a party of ladies and I cannot disturb her."

"Weel," said Thomson, pushing the servant aside and stepping into the hall. "Tell her I'm here."

Realising that the situation was beyond him, the servant sat Thomson down on a gimcrack little chair and told the Marchioness. She was delighted and excused herself to the ladies. She came down to have a chat with Thomson who brought her up to date with all the clash of the countryside including the saga of the keeper's big sow.

"Dae ye mind Sandy's big soo? Weel, she farrowed last week."

"Oh, how splendid," said the Marchioness.

"Aye," said Thomson, "She'd thirteen piglets."

"How marvellous," said the Marchioness. "Sandy would be pleased."

"Aye," said Thomson, "but that's no the hale o' it. She'd only twelve tits."

"Dear me," said the Marchioness, trying to keep control of the conversation. "All these piglets and only twelve teats. What did the thirteenth piglet do?"

"Oh," said Thomson, "it just sat doon on its doup and waited for a drink. Just like me."

The tinker man and woman were having a furious battle by the roadside. A passer-by asked what the dispute was about.

"There's nae dispute here," said the tinker, "We're baith o' the same mind. She thinks I have some money as she wants it and she thinks I'll no gie her ony an I agree wi' her."

A Glasgow man came into a lot of money and treated himself to a world tour. Wherever he went, Paris, Rome, Athens, Istanbul, Cairo, Jerusalem, Calcutta, Singapore, Melbourne, Wellington, San Francisco, New York, he stoutly averred that Glasgow was a bigger and better city in every way. When he arrived back home, he walked around studying the centre of Glasgow and was heard to say to himself, "Oh, whit a bliddy lee."

*　　*　　*

But it is in his jokes about religion that the Scot comes fully alive to produce some of his wittiest and most biting commentaries:

The Aberdeen landlady answered the knock on her door. It was just before the new university term and a young student wanted to know if she had a room. The landlady looked at him severely for a moment or two and then said, "Weel, if you're in maidicine or engineerin', ye can come in. But if you're ane o' thae drunken sweerin deeveenities, I dinna want ye."

At the time when Kirkintilloch was dry, it was the custom for thirsty citizens to spend all the permitted hours on Saturday in a nearby town slaking themselves thoroughly against the drought which was to face them on their return on the Sunday.

One such citizen had some difficulty in walking home and was overcome by a great alcoholic weariness as he took a short cut through the graveyard in the town. He fell asleep on one of the gravestones and lay in a deep stupor until nine o'clock on Sunday morning, a beautiful morning with a blinding sun shining down. At that moment, the Salvation Army band, with a great clashing of cymbals and a blaring of trumpets, burst into music. At the sudden sound, the sleeper, starting up to the blaze of the sun and the blast of the trumpets, looked around him at the rest of the gravestones and was heard to say, "Praise the Lord. But it's a gey puir turnoot for Kirkintilloch."

Two young boys were arguing about what they had been learning at Sunday school

"Aye, there's a devil."

"No, there's no."

"Aye, there is. It's just like Santa Claus. It's yer faither."

The bright-eyed Salvation Army lass shook her collection box under the nose of Sandy and invited him to give a donation to the Lord.

"Weel noo, ma lassie," said Sandy, "I'm a gey bit aulder nor you an I'll likely see the Lord afore ye, sae I'll juist wait an gie it tae him masel."

The woman in Brigton, Glasgow, was very moved by wee Willie's passing and she described the scene to a neighbour:

"There was wee Willie lyin in his bed wi' his big blue een and his fair curly hair lookin like a wee angel.

"'Maw,' he said in his wake wee voice, 'Wid ye gie me ma wee Oarange sash and ma wee Oarange drum.'

"So they pit the wee Oarange sash roon his wee shouthers and they gied him the wee Oarange drum and the wee drumsticks. He gied the drum wan wake wee tap wi' his wake wee fingers an said, 'Tae Hell wi' the Pope,' an passed straight tae the arms o' Jesus. Wasn't that a wonderful end!"

Another superior tourist looked round superciliously at a bonny douce wee village in Angus and said to Sandy, "What on earth do you find to do here when it rains?"

"We juist dinna interfere," replied Sandy.

It is appropriate to close this chapter with a celebrated joke, perhaps the perfect example of the Caledonian Calvinist humour which can point a moral and smile grimly at the same time.

148

The minister was flailing the congregation for their slackness. They were, he said, doomed by their sloth and sin to end up in the burning fiery pit.

"Ye'll be doon there in the pit amang the flames an there'll be weepin and wailin and gnashin o' teeth an ye'll say then, 'Lord, Lord, we didna ken' an the Lord, in His infinite wisdom an in His infinite mercy will look doon on ye, an He'll say, 'Weel, ye ken, noo'."

CHAPTER EIGHT

Cuimhnichibh na daoine o'n d'thainig sibh—
Remember the men from whom you came.

IN the past thirty years or so there has been a remarkable development of the facilities for adventuring today in Scotland. Before the war those who pioneered canoeing, skiing and pony-riding did so the hard way with little background support. For instance, in the thirties I was engaged with Leslie Ker Robertson in a weekly adventure series for the B.B.C. The concept was that we would take a beginner out each week-end and introduce him to a new outdoor adventure. One of these week-ends involved a three-day pony ride through the Trossachs. That was before the name "pony-trekking" was thought of and it was also before there was any understanding or organisation of the stabling facilities; the hardest part of our B.B.C. adventure series was finding the stabling each night.

We kept reminding ourselves that some day the glens and the hills and the rivers and the lochs would be better utilised. We yearned to see the water power used, the empty glens stocked.

Well, as a consequence of the devoted work by many enthusiasts, the dreams and aspirations have been realised. There is a remarkable structure of various bodies and individuals co-ordinated through the Scottish Council of Physical Recreation (now the Scottish Sports Council). Holiday adventure of all kinds and all the year round is superbly organised in Scotland and it is probably true to say that it is better equipped with expert organisers and enthusiasts than are the other parts of the British Isles. There has been a spontaneous expansion of effort.

My old friend, Leslie Ker Robertson to whom I referred above, for some years along with Jean, his wife, owned the Dunvegan Hotel, Isle of Skye, from which he operated pony-trekking, boating, salmon and sea fishing. He catered for a wide range of colourful and adventurous holidays, in addition to running, with his capable wife, a hotel with good food and good wine. Leslie was not always a hotelier and his own story has its own share of risk and courage. Although at first he was a banker, he took up journalism and, for a time, was a struggling freelance journalist. The phrase is a cliché but there are few freelance journalists for whom life is not a tough struggle to find the ideas and to sell them when found. It was while he was a freelance, helping to promote the Empire Exhibition in Bellahouston in Glasgow, that he and Jean were married and I was there in attendance as best man. That was in 1938. Fortunately, when the Exhibition closed, Leslie went on to the staff of the *Glasgow Evening News*. After war service in which Leslie was commissioned into the Glasgow Highlanders and Jean was commissioned in the A.T.S., Leslie returned to the *News*. In passing, it was a matter of wry amusement to Jean and me when we compared notes on our OCTU interviews to find that we had both been asked the same silly irrelevant question. "What games do you play?" they asked her: Jean who had earned her living as a secretary in the Linen Agency with its world-wide correspondence, and who had learned budgetting, cooking and housekeeping the hard way. In my own case, I had completed the standard questionnaire in which my listing of canoeing, climbing and camping must have made it clear that my spare time was fully utilised. It was sad that the officer selection technique, which had been so much improved, still seemed predicated on the assumption that the Battle of Waterloo was won on the playing fields of Eton. In Scotland, we incline to the view that the guns made by the Carron Company and which were known as carronades might well have exercised more influence. That, and the charge of the Gordon Highlanders clinging to the stirrups of the Royal Scots Greys were based on an older and tougher concept of life and death than the playing of any game.

In due course, Leslie took the road to Fleet Street. He became Assistant Editor of the *Daily Sketch* and concurrently used his abundant surplus energy in one of the first weekly disc programmes put out on the ITV channels. It was a busy demanding life but he hankered for north of the Border and personal independence. He sold up and, with a pocketful of money, headed for home. He and Jean went hotel-hunting and were tempted once or twice but, fortunately, did not commit themselves until the Dunvegan Hotel came on the market. Jean's people came from Skye so the Dunvegan had a sentimental pull, but it is also a good hotel which the pair of them made better year by year.

Their choice also had a sentimental flavour for me, too. I had known a previous proprietor, John MacDonald, one of the best types of hard-working Skyemen. He started in the hotel as boot boy, saved his money and his tips, and ended up as owner. When I knew him, he was retired and living in Edinburgh. On Princes Street with his homburg, cravat and butterfly-wing starched collar, he looked like any of the other prosperous citizens cushioned by prudent investment over the years—his first reading each morning was the financial news in *The Scotsman* to see how his shares were faring. In the evening at home, he kept himself busy. Hung around his neck and resting on his chest was a leather beetle into which he could stick the spare knitting needle while he knitted pairs of socks

155

for the old people in his home village of Drynoch in Skye. It was a remarkable sight and memorable to see year-round effort rather than a quick visit round the shops going into that Christmas minding. Although he was a man with a brisk mind and was a fast English speaker, he was, like all the Highlandmen of his day, more at home in his native tongue to which he reverted in times of stress. Describing his annoyance at something, the way he emphasised his irritation was to say, "I can tell you, I talked to myself in Gaelic for a long time afterwards."

Later, to my great delight, I found through John MacDonald a link with one of my Canadian colleagues. I was having dinner in Edinburgh with Ian H. MacDonald of Toronto, then vice-chairman of the Thomson newspaper empire in Canada. He was combining business with holiday and I asked him if he knew the Dunvegan Hotel. His reply startled me. "I ought to," he said, "I was born there." Up to that point I had assumed he was, as with so many Scots in Canada, several generations removed. It was a pleasure to tell him of my affection and respect for his father who, though successful in achieving a comfortable competence, was nevertheless, like so many of his contemporaries, a tough and uncompromising moralist who was no stricter with others than he was with himself.

In many ways this is still the factor which gives a different flavour to life in Scotland. It is this tougher attitude of mind which I like to think is still characteristic.

There can, of course, be shattering demonstrations of folly, of unawareness of personal and national background, of an ignorance of the vigorous Biblical language and thought in which generations have been reared. Television interviewers with their roving cameras would appear to have an unerring instinct for choosing the most illiterate and incoherent person on the street, and usually one whose speech is so slovenly and decayed that the rest of us squirm in humiliation at the sight and sound. And yet, and yet, even through some of these unrepresentative interviews one can sense behind the illiteracy a vigour of mind. For it is still true that, on the Northern side of the Border, the disputatious Scot lives on to enjoy talking, arguing, discussing. As a consequence, visitors and natives alike find themselves engaged in robust discussions of a kind which would be unusual south of the Border.

My old friend David Stephen is a case in point. He is a field naturalist with a world-wide reputation and, happily, he is not without honour in his own country. The new town of Cumbernauld, with commendable percipience and to their great credit, gave him a free hand to make their Palacerigg Country Park. He has brought a lifetime of understanding and imagination to his vision of recreating a habitat for the natural life of an area over which he ranged as a youth and which was the setting for his books on the fox and the roe deer. No one can be in David Stephen's company for long without recognising that he has an informed mind and that he will express that mind with uncompromising assertion. With the young of the wild and with children he has immense patience but he expects the adult human to talk and behave like a homo sapiens and he can be rough and unforgiving to those who do not so talk and behave.

I personally welcome the intellectual vigour and mental clash which comes as a fresh delight to the returning Scot. It gives to me the greater zest and is the greater savour to the adventure of life. The physical opportunities abound and for that we must count ourselves among the most fortunate, but my deepest thanks are for the daily recognition that here are

157

a people and a country where the adventures of the mind have always counted for more than the physical hardihood which so many of our people have abundantly demonstrated.

It is this quality of mind and character, which was greatly prized and which was always stressed, that we must cherish devotedly to-day when it is so much under attack and when it is so much needed.

It is my firm conviction that there is a special burden on the Scot. Just as the Jew became a vehicle for the clarification of the concept of God and for one of the most magnificent collections of religious prose and poetry so has the Scot become a vehicle for the expression of the concept of freedom in a determined personal independence of mind. That dedication to freedom goes back a long time in history. Tacitus put into the mouth of Calgacus, the Caledonian chief at the battle of Mons Graupius, a speech to his warriors as they faced the Roman legions, in which he said, "We are the people who never crouched in bondage." Calgacus lost that battle but the Romans, who had subdued Europe, conceded final defeat when they built Antonine's and Hadrian's walls to keep out the Caledonians they could not conquer. On the Wallace statue in Union Terrace, Aberdeen, one of the inscriptions is a quotation from his trial for treason in Westminster in the closing years of the 13th century: "To Edward King of England I cannot be a traitor. He is not my king. I owe him no allegiance. He has never received homage from me and, while life is in this persecuted body, he never shall receive it." That was to Edward I. A quarter of a century later—in 1320—in answer to the claim to the Pope by Edward II that Scotland was a vassal state in rebellion, there was sent to the Pope the stirring Declaration of Arbroath in which it was affirmed of King Robert Bruce "who has delivered us from the enemy. But should he at any time forsake us and swear allegiance to the English we will immediately disown him and choose another to rule over us. For so long as a hundred of us remain alive we will never submit to the domination of England. For it is not for riches or honour or glory that we fight but for that freedom which no good man loses but with his life."

A stirring declaration indeed and the continuing tradition was restated in many ways by Robert Burns, who emphasised the importance of freedom of mind in individual terms. As in the democratic basis of the proud reminder of Calgacus and in the Arbroath Declaration, so too did Burns make the point that freedom was not in the power or patronage or tyranny of the big battalions. As long as it exists in the heart and mind of even one man, it is a flame which can never be extinguished.

During the last war there was a joke in Scotland on that very theme. One by one the nations of Europe went down under the Nazis until France fell and we had the evacuation from Dunkirk. At that time, a Jock in a Glasgow pub was heard to say, "I suppose the next thing we'll hear will be that the English have packed it in as well and then we'll be on our own."

I doubt if the man who cracked the joke or those who repeated it could have told much in accurate detail of their country's story, or for that matter their own, but the tradition it expressed was rooted far back in history and its sentiment flowed in their blood stream.

It is a consequence of these formative historical forces that the Scot has been variously described as disputatious, determined, dour, and perhaps more than a little guilty from time to time of the sin of pride. Yet there is cause for proper pride which need not exclude proper humility.

159

Our patron saint, Andrew the fisherman, whose feast-day is the 30th of November, has a splendid special Mass which ought to give increased pride and pleasure to the members of the aulder and the newer kirks who may hear or read it. Look at these excerpts:

To me Thy friends, O God, are made exceedingly powerful; their power is become very great.

Yea, verily, their sound hath gone forth into all the earth, and their words unto the ends of the world.

Thou shalt make them princes over the whole earth . . . therefore shall the people praise Thee.

It is small wonder that, having been reared on a diet like that until the Reformation, the Scot tends to feel he has a few special qualities. The toughening four centuries with its Caledonian brand of Calvinism which followed enhanced that feeling. Nevertheless humility and humanity go with the pride. The Scot may often appear over-anxious to teach but he is always ready to learn and, although he may affect a superiority over the English, his guid conceit o' himsel' and his pride of race do not make him a racialist. His appreciation of the significance of personal qualities make him a natural egalitarian who recognises with his national poet that rank is an inessential and that the important factor is the quality of the man inside the trappings.

It is this and the continuing emphasis on personal liberty which gives grounds for the fascinating speculation of the implications inherent in a joint share in St Andrew with Russia and Greece. The Scot, dedicated as he is to the principle of independence of mind, might well be the man most fitted to help the people of the dictatorships of the left and the right to reassert the dignity inherent in the freedom to think and speak without fear or favour.

Lest I give the impression that I am an anglophobe, let me tell some of the story of a Canadian whose origin was in Leicester yeoman stock and of which he was very proud. J. W. Hobbs came to grips with a problem in stages. He bought a distillery in Fort William at the end of the war. His wife looked at the distillery manager's house and made it known that nothing would persuade her to live in it. So Joe Hobbs looked around. Inverlochy Castle with its estate came on the market and he bought it. Inverlochy Castle had been used as a commando training centre and by a Polish commando at that. Now, as most people know, when the army requisitions a big house, that house is stripped of carpets, floor coverings, everything that is perishable or a link with civilised living. The brutal and licentious soldiery then find themselves billeted in a bare shell of what was once but is now no longer a comfortable setting, bereft of all the small things which can help to restore an impression of homeliness. So they cannot well be blamed if they pin pictures or notices to the walls with nails or even bayonets. Nor is it entirely their fault if the constant clumping of heavy boots on bare floors and staircases erodes the historic patina. Nor, indeed, can they be blamed if they grow weary of the cold paleness of marble fireplaces and frescoes to the point where they attempt to bring warmth and life back by painting marble noses and marble breasts blue and red.

You will understand, then, that Joe Hobbs had a problem in retrieving Inverlochy Castle from its army trauma and bringing it back to acceptable standards. By then, however, he had a distillery maintenance squad and he put them on to the renovation of the castle and a marvellous job they made of it. When they had completed their work, Inverlochy was one of the most comfortable of the Highland houses in which to spend a night. It was also the one Highland house with the most perfect view in the whole of Scotland. In front of the portico is the whole western massif of Ben Nevis, standing there in all its great bulk and glory, impressive in the changing colours of the seasons from the fresh greens of spring to the browns of autumn and the glittering clean crispness of the winter snow.

But there was more than a view. The Inverlochy estate went nearly twenty miles up the glen to Spean Bridge and there were some 14,000 acres of unused glen and hillside. First of all, Hobbs thought of it as a potential outlet for the draff from the distillery as cattle food, but as he read and studied more his horizons expanded. He read that the glens and hillsides he now owned had carried a large herd of cattle and horses up to the time of Cumberland's despoliation in 1746 and onwards. He read of the figures running into thousands of cattle and horses rounded up on Cumberland's orders, and then he looked at his empty land where in all the vast acreage there were fewer than seventy cattle. He realised that the previous land usage dictated by experience of climate and terrain was one of pastoral farming.

He studied the problem in some depth and then decided to reverse the gradual decline and decay by starting beef cattle rearing on a big scale. In the course of his reading he had found that the general climatic conditions in the west of Ireland were similar to those in his part of the Great Glen. He decided that he would buy his basic stock in Ireland. He was a natural and flamboyant publicist. He called his enterprise The Great Glen Cattle Ranch. From the start he intended that the cattle—calves and all—should be out all the year. There were not enough trees to provide bad-weather shelter so he built three large open cement shelters. Characteristically he built them near the road where they were bound to be seen. He painted them a vivid yellow as he did all the farm buildings on the estate. Then he painted in large black letters on the roadside walls of the shelters: "Great Glen Cattle Ranch. Shelter No. 1, Shelter No. 2, Shelter No. 3."

Each year, as the herd increased, the hillsides grew greener from the presence of the cattle. He re-opened a lime quarry and limed and reseeded vigorously. In the development, he was lucky to have an enthusiast as his factor. Charlie Palmer threw all his energies into supporting Joe Hobbs and in a period of ten years they brought the number of cattle on the ranch up to 800 breeding cows and heifers, and when the calving time was on there could be as many as 1300/1400 cattle on the ground which ten years before supported fewer than 70. To provide winter keep, Hobbs and Palmer grew comfrey and made great pits of silage. They increased the arable acreage from some 67 acres to over 600 acres.

It was quite a saga as a physical achievement but the significant accolade was given at the sale ring by farmers from all over the country.

I attended several of the sales and watched other farmers' beasts auctioned but, in each case, when the first parcel of Great Glen calves was announced there was a new buzz of interest. When they went into the ring, they seemed to my amateur eye to look fitter and healthier than the previous lots. The farmers thought so, too, and proceeded to bid briskly at higher prices. As I say, that was the accolade for Hobbs— his imagination was brought to living achievement in hundreds of lusty young black beef beasts, and hard-headed tight-

163

fisted farmers proved him right with money from their rarely-opened pockets.

Joe Hobbs owned a large motor yacht whose hull had been built at the end of the war and was intended, he told me, for military river service in the Far East. But with the war over it was completed as a yacht and Hobbs bought her. She was a magnificent ship whose engines could be controlled from the bridge. He was very proud of her until he made a trip to Norway in heavy weather and came back with the plates in her side rippled where they had bent to the force of the waves. He was disgusted and sold it, only to buy another ship with a similar history. This one had been intended as a naval craft of trawler design but was not built by 1919. It too was finally completed as a private yacht but it had plates three-quarters of an inch thick compared with the other's three-eighths, and it had the most marvellous triple-expansion steam engine. Given plenty of water and plenty of coal it was an engine that could have gone on for ever.

On one of my visits I called in on Charlie Palmer for a quick chat but he told me that the "old man" knew I was in the area and wanted to talk to me. What Hobbs wanted was to ask me if I would keep him company on the steam yacht at the week-end when he was taking her down to the Clyde for overhaul. Needless to say, I promptly rearranged my time-table to join him.

The journey from Fort William to Oban was a delight but at Oban the weather forecast was ominous with conditions worsening to a south-easterly gale. As we went down the east coast of Kintyre it was clear that Hobbs did not relish the prospect of going round the Mull of Kintyre in the dark and in a gale. He eventually decided to anchor in West Loch Tarbert for the night. No one aboard liked the idea. Just a few weeks before, one of MacBrayne's ships, whose captains and crews know every inch of the western coastline, had gone aground in the same place. In addition, the chart showed that the loch was filthy with rocks, skerries and shoals. Hobbs nosed in carefully at half-speed until Angus, a deckhand from Islay, who was standing outside, pipe in mouth and leaning against the bridge housing, took his pipe out of his mouth and said calmly, pointing dead ahead, "There's a patch of white over there, Mr Hobbs, and I think it's a rock." Everyone shot to the rail to peer but it was quite unnecessary. Angus had phenomenal eyesight and it was a rock. Hobbs reduced speed again and we crawled in. Then Angus, still leaning against the bridge housing, took his pipe out of his mouth again and just as calmly, dispassionately even, as if he were an observer standing safely on shore, said, "To tell you the truth, Mr Hobbs, I don't think ye can anchor here at all."

He was right, although we did anchor on that sandy lee shore but it was with anchors fore and aft, and one or two people had the wind up. The engineer let it be known that he intended to stay on watch all night and keep up a head of steam in case the anchors dragged. The cook, who was an east-coaster from north of Aberdeen, declared mutinously as he peeled the potatoes, "If we'd a quaalified skipper aboard we widna' be in here." That was a bit unfair for Hobbs knew his seamanship, but it was indicative of the strain. There were two other friends of Hobbs aboard and they stayed up all night chain-smoking nervously. I discovered next morning that I was the only one who turned in and had a good sleep. I found it easy. Years of journalism had taught me a useful discipline which army training had reinforced; when you have completed your part of the task and have handed it over to the next man, separation of function and responsibility

165

demands that you leave him to the work which is now out of your hands. Although newspaper work has cost me a lot of sleep over the years, I owe it that good night's rest in the gale in West Loch Tarbert.

We were delivered safely in Glasgow, and six weeks later Hobbs invited me to accompany him from the Clyde back to Fort William. It was idyllic weather. The ship, the sea, the islands, the crew smiled all week-end in the sun and West Loch Tarbert as we passed it looked innocent, inviting and beautiful.

Joe Hobbs and Charlie Palmer are both dead now but when you tour the British Isles and see groups of black cattle on moorland hills, where previously there would have been only sheep, raise your hat in salute to their memory. Many of the beasts you see undoubtedly owe their presence there to-day to Joe Hobbs, an Anglo-Canadian whose final adventure restored life to dying glens and is still bringing life back to bare hillsides. Indeed there was a strangely fortuitous timing to his cattle-ranching venture and its impact on the food production potential of Scotland and, for that matter, many areas in England and Wales. He pointed the way back to the proper and historical use of marginal land with the result that, to-day, we are physically better at rearing more beef beasts and we are now psychologically attuned to the change. We could hardly be better placed to provide the European Common Market with the quality beef and mutton which they cannot rear in quantity on their pastures but which we can produce in vastly increased tonnages.

The development of the North Sea oil fields will have more effect on Scotland than elsewhere in Britain. Already the impact is being felt but, as in the case of outdoor sport so in the case of industry, we have the bodies in existence which will organise the exploitation in socially acceptable terms. Foremost among these is the Scottish Council (Development and Industry) which began as a voluntary body doing the promotional selling for Scottish industry which ought to have been done by the Board of Trade. It is a job which the Scottish Council is still doing as a consequence of a self-help drive which began in Glasgow between the wars as the Glasgow Development Council. Sometimes our M.P.s. Provosts and others engage in public whining and begging (and sometimes it may well be necessary) but that should not be allowed to obscure the enormously successful independent action which is being conducted in so many spheres. In the north-east of England I have heard envious references to the unity of purpose of the various Scottish lobbies. While I am secretly pleased to hear these references I am, of course aware of the fissiparity which is so often a concomitant of our individual independence. On the other hand, my sometimes quarrelsome compatriots will be flattered to know that the impression they create is one of determined unity.

I am fortunate in that I have a wide circle of friends in all walks of life and in different countries who will understand exactly what I mean when I sum up what I have written in a somewhat uncompromising and even dogmatic statement:

The strong moral qualities which earned the Scot respect throughout the world and throughout history were based on deep religious convictions. We ought to remind ourselves that we cannot succeed to the respect given to our forefathers if we turn away from the qualities and the convictions which made our fathers great. They did not build their reputation for character and self-discipline by running away from life's problems and its battles. I am persuaded that they would have unhesitatingly spurned today's limp heresy which suggests

167

that the solution to the moral dilemmas is to be released from any need to choose the difficult. The permissive society citizen claims the right to do as he chooses and then he demands that society absolve him from the consequences of his own actions. Our fathers had a firmer concept of personal responsibility and would have rejected that kind of permissiveness as unworthy. They would have re-asserted belief in the basic qualities which go to make the man, which give security and serenity to a family, and which confer stability on a nation.

In a world of shifting values, a world which has rarely seen so sustained an assault on the moral standards as there is today, we owe it to our children to pass on to them what we ought to have learned from our fathers; the Scot who does not have somewhere within his soul an awareness of the importance of the abiding values is only half a Scot, for the adventure of life must not be directed only to the physical. It encompasses also the challenges of the intellect and spirit, wherein the greater victories lie. That is the enduring and the constant challenge in any land where there is an understanding of life and the adventure which it can bring.